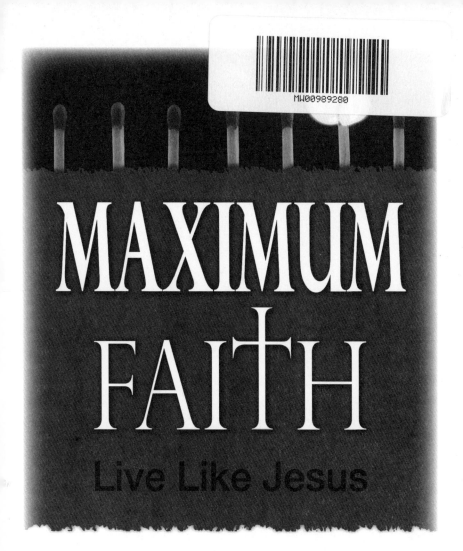

MAXIMUM FAI†H

Live Like Jesus

Experience Genuine Transformation

GEORGE BARNA

Visit the Maximum Faith website at www.maximumfaith.com.

Maximum Faith: Live Like Jesus
Copyright © 2011 by George Barna. All rights reserved.

ISBN: 978-0-9831729-0-1

Published in association with the literary agency of Fedd and Company, Inc.
606 Flamingo Blvd., Austin, TX 78734

A joint publication of Metaformation Inc., Ventura, California; Strategenius Group LLC, New York, New York; and WHC Publishing, Glendora, California.

Designer: Lamp Post Inc.
Editor: Anita K. Palmer

MAXIMUM FAITH

Live Like Jesus

GEORGE BARNA

CONTENTS

SECTION 3
ROLL UP YOUR SLEEVES

APPENDICES

PREFACE

Reader alert! This book has an odd structure. You may not have encountered any book quite like it. However, there's a reason for it. It's based on research I conducted concerning how people read books.

It turns out that most people finish about one third of any book they start reading. If that's correct, then a significant share of those who open this book will probably give up before reaching the halfway mark — and that challenges me to try something different. Sticking with the traditional approach to structuring book content — i.e., set up the problem, present the options, and offer a solution — won't produce the desired results. (If you think about it, no wonder Americans are reading less these days: if we only read the first portion of a book, all we keep reading about are the problems we face, with no solutions. How depressing is that!)

While reflecting on this curiosity, it dawned on me that the Bible, perhaps anticipating this challenge, teaches about life in three ways: principles, practices, and prescriptions. Take, for example, evangelism — the process of telling people who are stuck in a life of sin and self-reliance that there is good news: God wants to forgive them and lead them on an amazing journey of discovery, intimacy, joy, and fulfillment. To help us understand that incredible opportunity, the Bible provides all three types of information for our consideration.

Sometimes we encounter evangelistic principles that are stated, straight out. An example is Peter speaking to the religious rulers in Acts 4:12, where he clearly states that salvation is through Jesus Christ alone, and people must know Him to be saved. Other times we gain insight into evangelistic practices, such as provided in Acts 5:41-42, in which the apostles ignored the physical abuse and verbal warnings of the religious officials and continued to preach the gospel everywhere possible. Alternatively, we sometimes receive prescriptions concerning outreach, like the one in Acts 4:29-30, where the assembled believers acknowledged the need to heal and preach with boldness in the name of Jesus.

DEVELOPING A READING PLAN

Wary of unintentionally failing to provide you with exposure to the proven solutions God has provided for us to reach our full potential, I have therefore divided this book into three intimately related but unique sections — not quite in thirds, but at least in three distinct portions. I encourage you to read all three sections, but if you are a "typical" reader, that's probably not your inclination. So, if you are going to read only part of the book, consider the following descriptions of each section and then develop your reading plan accordingly.

Section 1: The first section is for those who want the facts and principles. If you want an overview of the challenges we face in optimizing our life's journey with God, a summary of the stops on the journey to maturity, information about the statistical frequency with which people reach each stop along that journey, and brief insights into what each stop on the journey entails, then be sure to read Section 1.

Section 2: The second section is for those who love a story — especially one that relates to our own lives and gives us good ideas for purposeful reflection and personal growth. This segment of the book is influenced greatly by the qualitative research conducted for the project. The story of Jennifer is a composite drawn from the case studies of people who have made serious progress on the transformational pathway. Her adventure with God reveals common battles and triumphs that people experienced as they moved toward completing the journey in all its fullness. The conversations, reflections, and activities Jennifer engages in are designed to give you some handles to grab onto in your own effort to optimize your life with God.

Section 3: The final section is not only the briefest, but also perhaps the most practical of all. It provides pragmatic ideas regarding what to do about the conditions and opportunities described earlier in the book. This section delivers hands-on action steps you can take to facilitate transformation in partnership with God — for your personal transformation as well as the journey to wholeness of other people within a church-driven context.

Let me reiterate that you are likely to receive the greatest benefit by reading the entire text. However, I am a realist. If you choose to not read *Maximum Faith: Live Like Jesus* from cover to cover, I trust that this design will enable you to grasp the main points in an efficient manner that best suits your interests.

INTRODUCTION

MAXIMUM FAITH.

Those simple words confound many people. It's not that we are afraid to discuss matters of faith. We commonly talk about personal faith, faith in the public square and marketplace, differences between various faith groups, fanatical faith, unreasonable faith, and even the beauty of a child's simple faith. But we squint with uncertainty — and maybe even discomfort — regarding the idea of maximum faith.

Make no mistake about it: Americans are a religious people, prone to attending religious events and belonging to communities of faith. But we are also a nation of religious people willing to settle for adequate or sufficient faith — instead of maximum faith. We hear that expressed as "I have enough faith to get by," or "I have all the faith I need" or "I have more faith than most people."

It's probably not too often that you hear or think about having maximum faith. Yet, that's the very reason God created you: for you to exercise maximum faith in Him and enjoy the results of that deep conviction and the altered lifestyle it inevitably produces.

GREAT CAPACITY FOR FAITH

Don't miss — or misunderstand — my point. I am not accusing you, or most Americans, of being faithless or of lacking enormous faith. Most Americans are people of substantial faith. It's simply a question of who or what we place our faith in, and how that faith shapes our lives. Think about common experiences and activities in your life; many of them reflect the objects of our faith.

- You have faith that the 2,000-pound piece of metal and glass you are guiding through space at 70 miles per hour — i.e., your car — will stop on command without crashing into the people and things in front of and around you.

- You have complete faith that an unseen force known as gravity will somehow keep you firmly and comfortably planted on a massive dirt clod (aka Earth) that is spinning at a rate of 1,000 miles per hour while simultaneously hurtling through the universe, in an orbit around the sun, at about 67,000 miles per hour. [1]

- You believe that if you extract the insides of a cow or chicken, expose it to a high enough temperature for a long enough period of time, and then eat it, your body will accept that offering as fuel, enabling you to stay healthy and active.

- You are convinced that a Boeing 747, which weighs in excess of 350,000 pounds, can rise above the earth and safely transport you eight miles above the ground at a speed of 550 miles per hour for more than half a day, and then safely come to a complete stop after hitting the ground at more than 100 miles per hour. [2]

- The same lake in which you swam during summer freezes over during winter. After a month of below-freezing temperatures you have no hesitation to skate across the lake, believing that the same fluid you swam through in July is now a solid that is strong enough to simultaneously bear your weight and that of many other people.

- You turn on your faucet and drink the liquid that emerges, believing it to be safe for your body, even though you don't know where it has come from or who put what chemicals, if any, in that water.

- Based on the recommendation of a person you believe has had extensive medical training, you allow that "doctor" to put a sharp needle through your skin to inject fluids into your body with the expectation that the chemical substances, most of whose names you cannot pronounce and about which you know next-to-nothing, will help your body to be healthier.

- You purchase numerous cans, bottles and packages from a grocery store and place the contents of those packages in your body, even though you do not know a single person in any of the companies that provided the contents, believing that the components listed on the packaging are accurate and safe.

Obviously, we have considerable faith in many people, gadgets and substances that we know little or nothing about. Clearly we have a great capacity for faith. The question is whether we have a deep, personal and growing faith in God, as well as the will to let Him transform us into the people He desires us to be.

"GOOD CHRISTIANS"

An objective assessment suggests that few Americans have maximum faith in God. As the data in subsequent chapters will reveal, literally tens of millions of American Christians have denied God His rightful place on the throne of our lives and withheld control of our lives so that we, not He, can reign supreme, all under the cover of being "good and responsible Christians."

In all likelihood your mind is now furiously racing to muster the information you need to persuasively challenge this allegation. Your defense begins by noting that by any reasonable measure you are a "good Christian."

You attend church, read the Bible, quote God's words, freely give money to worthy causes, and bring your children to Sunday school and church youth group meetings. You readily acknowledge that you have sinned against God and asked for His forgiveness; you believe that He answers (or at least hears) your prayers; and you are wont to tell people in trouble they must turn to God. You believe orthodox Christian teachings, such as those regarding the eternal, holy, omniscient, and omnipotent nature of God; the creation of the world by God; the virgin birth; Jesus's crucifixion and resurrection; the reliability and authority of the Bible; and the wise, loving, and unstoppable involvement of God in the world today. In your mind there is no question whatsoever: Christianity is the best and only viable faith in existence, and you are personally committed to it.

You are, by your own unflinching testimony, a Christian — a Christ-follower.

Say what you will, but there is about a 94 percent probability that even as you read this, you remain an active participant in a continuing rebellion against the holy God of Israel. Like alcoholics who think that one drink won't affect them, you and I have convinced ourselves that our inability to see ourselves for who we really are and to give God total control of all aspects of our lives is a natural and common failing, a weakness that is both predictable and expected. We admit that we're not perfect; we have flaws and we still sin. Yet we are good people, godly people, and we are confident that we are consistently becoming more like our savior Jesus Christ. And we prayed the "Sinner's Prayer," so we are "right with God" and sure of our eternal salvation. As we observe the moral decline of our society, we are confident that we are not part of the problem; we are exemplars of His kingdom.

But despite all the self-recommending activities we list or the theological truths we know and intellectually believe, make no mistake about it: the evidence clearly identifies us as brothers and sisters in arms, quietly rising up in steadfast opposition to the God who loves us more than we presently understand.

Thankfully, there is good news despite this dark cloud of accusation. Our resistance has failed to take God by surprise. In fact, it has been anticipated, understood and forgiven by God. He is so in love with us, His master creation, that He willingly sacrificed a part of Himself so that we could have an unending relationship with Him.

We, in response and realizing that our alternative was not too attractive, invited Him to reside in our hearts, accepting the special gift of love and forgiveness that He offered, along with His promise of eternal salvation. But then, in an act of stealth sedition, once we felt certain that we had His gift securely in hand, we abandoned Him and continued to pillage and plunder the world in search of earthly treasures and pleasures.

We pulled the old double-cross on the One who died for us on the old rugged cross.

True to His grace-giving nature, though, He will forgive our years of self-reliance, self-indulgence, selfishness, continual sin, and refusal to worship Him alone. Despite how we have abused Him, much as His Son was abused on earth for our sake almost 2,000 years ago, He remains eager to move forward into a deeper relationship with us. He contends that we are redeemable; it is still possible for us to become the loving, worshiping, obedient disciples that we were placed on earth to become.

Yes, He is still seeking to bestow the full riches of His kingdom on you and me. He is willing to overlook the fact that those of us who are allegedly "born-again Christians" have behaved like adulterous lovers, succumbing to the charms and lures of this world while believing that we are protected by an irrevocable eternal fire insurance policy that has been signed, sealed and delivered by God Himself.

If we are honest with ourselves, we know that we suffer from occasional lapses of self-doubt. We have secretly wondered where that "peace that surpasses all understanding" could be found. Or where we might get our hands on that joy that is the reward of devout followers of Christ. And what about that all-encompassing love that is supposed to be the signature piece of our character, the one by which others will know us? You see, deep down — well, not really too deep — we know that something is missing, something is off. We may be happy, but we lack joy; we may be satisfied but we're not fulfilled; we might feel at ease, but not truly content.

God's continuous grace is indeed good news for those of us who have been seeking peace from the wrong places, practices, people and perspectives. Genuine peace and fulfillment is within our grasp — if we will simply abandon our self-defeating ways and return to the path of righteousness on this lifelong journey to wholeness.

In other words, the best is yet to come — if we are willing to let God transform us His way.

SIX YEARS OF RESEARCH

Wait! Before you cast this book aside and say that it's not written for you, that I've got the wrong person, that this is a case of mistaken identity — after all, you would never consciously rebel against the God who sent His Son to die for your salvation, and you resent such an accusation — give me a chance to describe what my most recent research about the state of our lives has revealed.

It took me six years to conduct and make sense of this research, and I think it explains many of the secret and sometimes confusing emotions, fears, experiences, disappointments, and frustrations that we encounter.

Even more so, this research gives us a simple and practical explanation of where we stand on life's journey and what we must do to move forward to optimize our God-given potential. If you consider yourself to be a Christian, then yes, this book is meant for you.

As a down payment on that claim, let me summarize where we will go in this book. At the risk of sounding presumptuous, this relatively brief volume might turn out to be one of the most helpful books you will read.

BEGINNING WITH QUESTIONS

Do you ever wonder if the life you're experiencing is really all there is to the victorious life that God promised you? Is this as good as it gets? Is this the totality of what Jesus died for you to experience?

Is your frustration with your church, your spiritual life, and even other Christians something more than just a dry spell in your faith walk?

When you read what Jesus and the apostle Paul had to say about living a transformed life, do you realize that despite years of effort and the best of intentions, somehow you have not arrived there? With that in mind, do you yearn to know and experience the profound richness of life, and the freedom and peace that they were describing?

When you tell somebody that you are a Christian, are you confident that your life is a loud and consistent testimony of the principles that Jesus taught His followers? Are you comfortable with the idea that if people imitate your life, they are also imitating the life of Christ? Do you ever feel embarrassed that perhaps you are not an appropriate poster child for the faith that you represent?

Have you ever given up on trying to pull your life together on your own terms and in your own power, and acknowledged that you are too broken to succeed on your own? Are you conscious of how God is healing you from the inner wounds you have hidden from others — and perhaps even from yourself? Have you turned to God and asked Him to do whatever He needs to do for you to become the whole and holy individual He birthed you to be?

When someone asks about your goals in life, do you rattle off human achievements you hope to accomplish, or do you describe outcomes that you believe are God's unique will for your life? Who really controls your life these days?

When you hear about the lives of "super saints" — people like Francis of Assisi, Brother Lawrence, Saint Augustine, John Wesley, John Wycliffe, Hudson Taylor, Corrie ten Boom, George Muller, Mother Teresa — do you believe that they displayed a kind of depth and otherliness that you could never hope to achieve? Do you look at them in awe and conclude that their relationship with God was unnatural and far beyond anything you believe is within your grasp?

Those are valid but sometimes difficult questions for contemporary American Christians to answer. They are the kinds of questions whose answers define the nature of your life — and your ability to experience all the greatness that God has in store for you. It is these kinds of questions — and the answers to them — that form the foundation of this book.

ALONG THE TRANSFORMATION JOURNEY

Based on research, how does God transforms lives, and how do we work with Him to facilitate transformational outcomes? Here, in a skeletal form, is the basic argument, which I will then restate and unpack in practical ways as we go along.

Life is a journey. Okay, big yawn; you already know that. But what you might not know — in fact, the research shows that few Christians in America do — is the itinerary for that journey: the stops along the way, what happens at each of those stops, and how to successfully navigate through the obstacles that you may encounter and keeping advancing while enjoying the journey.

You'll find the statistical support for the following claims in chapters two and three. For now, consider the following:

Most Americans consider themselves to be Christian.

A majority of Americans, however, never make a confession and profession of faith in which they invite Jesus Christ to save them from the penalty of their sins against God. They are not, in other words, "born-again Christians."

Even among the born-again population, only a tiny proportion get beyond their profession of faith to experience the more robust and significant outcomes that are made available by Christ to His followers.

A major reason why few of us experience the richness of the

Christian life is because we do not know what to do beyond reading and memorizing more Bible verses, attending church services more consistently, donating larger sums of money to worthy causes, volunteering a few hours at church, and discussing our faith in Jesus with family and friends.

A majority of believers who figure out where the journey goes, and what it takes to maximize the opportunity God grants us by completing the journey to wholeness, instead choose to settle for a less complete and fulfilling life.

If you are like me and tens of millions of other church-going Christians in the United States, it is difficult to be honest about the real nature of your current relationship with God and where it is headed. In all likelihood, an objective assessment would label that relationship "active but stalled." It need not stay on its current plateau, but we are not making much progress in moving ahead to exploit the richer possibilities that are available to us.

HOW WE PLAY TUG-OF-WAR

As we will see in the pages that follow, there are a handful of fundamental issues in this tug-of-war we wage with the Father who has spared us from what we truly deserve. Discussions about these matters will be featured in coming chapters. But here is what we'll dig into.

The first issue relates to *desire*. When we experience a state of disturbing spiritual discontent, which most of us do after a while, our response depends upon how much we really want to connect at the deepest possible level with God. Like everything else, it's a choice we make; He never forces us to go deep with Him. You might be surprised by what the research shows about this stage in our spiritual development.

Another issue concerns *humility*. Like a wild stallion running free and recklessly through fields and canyons, we refuse to be broken. We may use some God talk, but in our hearts and minds, life is all about us.

The idea of being a broken person whom only God can fix sounds good theologically, but we want nothing to with it personally. And until we are broken of ourselves, God doesn't have much to work with.

And then there's the matter of *control*. Simply put, we have it and we stubbornly refuse to hand it over to God. He could take it from us in a heartbeat, but that's not how true love works, so He doesn't confiscate what is rightfully His. He just waits for us to give it to Him. Sadly, the longer we resist, the more we lose out. Despite our words to the contrary, we have refused to surrender our will in favor of His, and to submit every aspect of our life to His lordship.

The final issues revolve around *love*. You knew it would come to that, didn't you? After all, that is the ultimate point of the journey: to so fully experience God's love that we are able to express a similarly profound love to both God and other people.

The apostle John wrote a gospel and several epistles communicating to the effect that "God is love." Not that He simply enjoys love, understands love, gives love, or is fascinated by love; He *is* love. And that is our ultimate calling as well.

Satan is committed to distracting us with cheap imitations of that love, outcomes such as happiness, satisfaction, achievement, contentment, fame, power, sexual gratification and the like. But the point of the journey is that we are made whole by freely and expansively receiving and reflecting true love, God's kind of love. We are made in His likeness and gifted with this ability. We have been exposed to the life of Christ and called to imitate it. We cannot simply gin up a warm feeling about God and people and say we have adequately accomplished our God-given calling.

SEEKING HOLINESS

In the final analysis, we are to be holy because God is holy. Throughout the Bible we are reminded that He invites, prepares, and exhorts us to be holy — not perfect but holy.

Holiness simply means being set apart by God for an astounding life of freedom and joy if we will live for Him and allow Him to live through us. Because you made that seemingly simple profession of faith, His Holy Spirit lives in you and enables you to experience the holy life. But we usually struggle to make headway in our relationship with God, which has a devastating effect on our spiritual growth and ultimate destiny. We will explore that more closely.

It has been said that if you don't know where you're going, any road will get you there — and our experience has proven that having good intentions without a sense of direction leads to disappointment and frustration. The rest of this book will therefore serve as a road map for your journey to wholeness — a guidebook designed to motivate us to end our unwinnable rebellion against a holy and loving Father and to help us arrive at the ultimate life destination that God has prepared for us.

God has not given up on us and will never give up on us. If we are willing to cooperate with Him and persevere on this transformational journey, He will supply all the help we need to make it to the final stop on the journey. But what is that stop? What are the stops along the way? How do we know where to go and how to get there?

To find out, keep reading — and don't forget to put on your seat belts for the ultimate joy ride.

STOPPING TO CONSIDER

Before we dig into this, here is a final caveat for you to consider. As you will discover in chapter three in the next section, the journey is divided into a pathway with *ten stops* — temporary resting places at which we are built up in preparation for the continuation of the journey. This book assumes that you have at least reached Stop 5 on this journey — that is, you have accepted Jesus Christ as your Lord and Savior and have engaged in the typical spiritual development activities that follow such a commitment (e.g., attending church services, reading the Bible, praying, etc.).

But perhaps you have not yet arrived at Stop 4 (which you'll learn is *Asking God to forgive you and send His Holy Spirit into your life*) and Stop 5 (which is *Engaging in spiritual development and outreach efforts that reflect your newfound love of Jesus Christ, your savior*). If you have not considered your need to be saved from sin and self, or perhaps have pondered the matter but have not asked Jesus Christ to be that savior you need, I invite you to do so before reading any further. The remaining contents of this book are built upon having made such a decision.

To understand the nature of that commitment, check out the resources at websites such as *www.crosswalk.com/who-is-jesus/christian-salvation* and learn more about the commitment that initiates the ultimate transformation of your life. If you choose to make such a commitment, then the material in this book will be a practical aid to moving forward in your new life in partnership with Jesus Christ. It will be the best decision you have ever made — and one whose benefits will be multiplied by understanding the journey described in these pages.

SECTION 1

ROAD MAP FOR THE JOURNEY

CHAPTER 1

THE TRANSFORMATION JOURNEY

*What counts is whether we have been transformed into a
new creation.*

— Galatians 6:15

WHAT GETS YOU OUT OF BED IN THE MORNING?

Why bother to shower, get dressed, fight the traffic, work your shift, answer texts and emails and phone calls, fight the traffic again, endure checkout lines, discipline the kids, pay bills, take care of the yard, exercise, maybe watch a little TV or a DVD — then hit the sack and hit the repeat button seven hours later? I'm not saying you shouldn't maintain your daily routine, or that there's anything wrong with what you're doing. But the fact that you keep doing it begs the question, why? What's your motivation? Why bother?

Or, phrased differently, have you ever felt like God must have intended for us to achieve more in this life than we're experiencing through our current lifestyle and choices?

Sometimes we get so buried in our routines — the efforts devoted to mere survival, never mind thriving — that we operate on auto-pilot and lose sight of the big picture. In fact, just getting through another day sometimes seems like the big picture! When the grand vision that defines our identity and dreams evaporates, we become victims of life rather than victors in life.

So let's take a deep breath and re-establish the portion of that big picture that we have in common.

When God created you, He created someone special — a one-of-a-kind person He loves without question and wants to share life with. He gave you life as a gift — one with a significant purpose. Like a caterpillar that morphs from the inside out into a beautiful and graceful butterfly, able to revel in freedom and beauty and to bring joy to those who experience it in motion, you were born with astounding purpose and potential.

That purpose is not to simply bull your way through eighty years of highs and lows with determination and grit. God created you with the expectation that you would achieve greatness. Not greatness as defined by the world — the fat bank account, majestic house, luxury cars, jet-set vacations, designer clothing, and the like. His notion of greatness relates solely to becoming the ultimate version of you that He envisioned. His vision focuses entirely on your commitment to loving Him and other people, and to experience incredible exhilaration and wonder in the midst of those relationships and shared experiences.

You were made to be successful. But in God's economy, success is achieved by loving God and people completely and creatively 24/7, not just when it is easy or convenient. Total fulfillment in life is delivered by loving comprehensively — that is, expressed through a blend of your heart (feelings), mind (thoughts), body (physicality), and soul (spirit). This kind of holistic love can only be experienced in cooperation with God, since it requires a contribution on our part as well as His. At the risk of giving Lennon and McCartney too much credit, it seems that they were onto something special when they sang "all you need is love."

We become easily confused by the simplicity of God's plan in our sophisticated world. What about physical accomplishments, financial ascendancy, intellectual superiority, global fame? Where do they rank on the scale of significance? None of those worldly goals even register as a blip on God's radar. More often than not, those are mere distractions in light of our God-given purpose. Until you invest yourself fully in achieving the kind of greatness He made you for, your life suffers from unrealized potential. [3]

When you commit yourself to pursuing that God-given purpose, you discover that it provides you with direction in life and a sense of value. That purpose, because it reflects your relationship with God, also establishes a significant part of your identity in Christ. And the more you dig into understanding and executing that purpose, the more meaningful it becomes for you. After all, as the desired outcomes emerge you also realize many of the promises of God, such as joy, peace, patience, hope, self-control and more. You find that there is an abundant freedom and sense of release that comes from your growing relationship with God, the perpetual presence of His Holy Spirit, and the power and wisdom that He provides to His true disciples.

Clearly, becoming this type of person demands a very different approach to life — different goals, different experiences, different self-assessment, and a different investment strategy related to the resources we control.

To facilitate your greatness, He has provided you with a unique journey — a set of relationships, opportunities, insights, and experiences unlike that which any other person in history has encountered. Your pilgrimage is not a reflection of random occurrences; it has been custom designed by the Creator of the universe specifically for you, in order to prepare you for a fulfilling and fruitful life. It is a journey with twists and turns you cannot predict and you cannot conquer alone. Only when you embark on the journey with Him by your side can you master its challenges and emerge victorious.

GOD-LOVE OR SELF-LOVE

So we return to the question we asked earlier: Why isn't your life shaping up as a victory parade that gets repeated every day? The answer is encompassed in three immense concepts described by just five short words: free will, spiritual warfare, sin.

God has always wanted us to recognize His greatness and His love for us, and hoped our response would be to fully commit our lives to Him. But, of course, if He forced us to love Him, it would not be genuine love, so He had to give us the opportunity to choose to love or not love Him — hence the infamous quality known as "free will."

It was that same capacity to choose God-love or self-love that led to the downfall of a rotten angel, whom we call Satan (aka the Devil). And that downfall led to the spiritual battle for our minds, hearts, bodies, and soul: should we devote ourselves to fully loving, obeying and serving ourselves or God? To our detriment, we have deployed that capability to distance ourselves from Him and His ways — i.e., choosing to offend God, which is known as sin. We "choose to refuse" to cooperate with God in His simple plan to enable us to make the most of our time on earth. Faced with the choice of operating in concert with God's ways or going it our own, we consistently choose the latter — against our best interests and His best plan.

Why do we do this? Because we have a problem — a spiritual maturation problem. God's ultimate plan for your life is for you to be transformed into a sterling imitation of Jesus Christ. [4]

The first significant exchange in the transformation process is to respond to His gracious offer of perpetual salvation, but that is merely the beginning of the real journey toward spiritual wholeness. To assist you in that journey He provides a role model (Jesus Christ), a 24/7 advisor (the Holy Spirit), an exhaustive but nontechnical document containing the critical plans, operating principles and performance metrics (the Bible), and a support group (the Church). If you use those resources appropriately, you will experience the kind of redefined life He has promised.

But in a stunning display of either arrogance or ignorance — or perhaps both — we consistently choose different role models, ignore our consultant, fail to read the manual, pursue our personal preferences and measures, and refuse the input and accountability available from the support group. The bottom line in God's eyes is whether or not we love Him. Sadly, over the last thirty years my research has invariably revealed that we give God world-class lip service but we follow the whims of our minds and hearts. We call on God only when we have to — when our plans have crashed and burned, when we are desperate, when we feel empty and hopeless, when even our best efforts are not good enough.

The result of our self-indulgence is that we lead lives of perplexity and frustration. We read about the promises of God, but don't experience their fulfillment. We participate in the institutionalized church, but find it less meaningful and satisfying than expected. We read the Bible, but generally lack a true understanding of the text, miss its richness, and misinterpret its counsel. We vacillate between the letter and the spirit of the Law, and receive the hope of neither. We take solace in being religious but overlook the value of true spirituality.

In essence we move from birth to exploration, self-determination, then desperation and wind up the journey pursuing either transformation or experiencing exasperation. Those of us who choose to seek authentic and holistic transformation do so because we realize we have abused the gift of free will by ignoring God's boundaries, preferring to do what we want rather than what God intended or commanded. Moved by that insight, we then wrestle with that awareness of and dismay over our sinful state and ask God to give us another chance, one in which we will consciously seek to follow His ways and rebuild our relationship with Him.

Most of the people I have interviewed for this book acknowledged that they recognized the consequences of their ill-advised choices, but were not sure what to do next. Attending more worship services proved not to be the answer, and neither was taking on more volunteer duties at the church. Our ignorance of the journey helps to explain why the research indicates that only a relative handful of people make serious progress on the journey to wholeness.

CHANGE OR TRANSFORMATION?

Change has become a big topic of conversation and study in our culture. Most of us think that we have the power to enforce meaningful change into our lives. Of course, we also believe politicians when they tell us they are going to change politics for the better. We know how that has worked out.

So let's begin our investigation of the transformation process that God brings to our lives by understanding that the term transformation is not synonymous with the word change. The two terms differ in scope and significance. You have undergone countless changes in your life, probably including many memorable spiritual changes, but it is not likely that you have experienced all of the spiritual transformation that God has in store for you.

Most people use these terms interchangeably. Let me explain the difference. Change is a refinement that is typically short-term, impermanent, incremental, superficial, and of limited ultimate consequence. In contrast, transformation is generally long-term, permanent, systemic, deep, and monumental in its impact and consequences. Change merely alters a known reality; transformation radically redefines that reality.

We are often uncomfortable with change but may grudgingly introduce some form of it to reshape part of our life — usually only when we are confident that it will improve our life in some measurable way. In contrast, we are typically incapable of even conceptualizing what our lives will be like when they are transformed. In most instances, we can imagine and then implement a series of changes in our lives. But transformation is beyond our capabilities; we have to partner with others who bring additional resources to the process.

Let me give you a few examples of this difference, because it's important that you grasp the significance if you are going to commit yourself to transformation, rather than settle for change.

If you switch your attendance from First Baptist Church to Cornerstone Christian Church, that's change. If you switch from trying to balance enjoying the world and being a decent, moral person to allowing God to have full control of your life every moment of every day, then you are pursuing a transformed life.

People who transition from having no church life to attending church services have undergone a meaningful change. Those who shift from joining, attending and promoting a church to *being* the Church — consistently living out the commands of Christ and actively seeking to represent Him in every thought, word and deed — have undergone a transformation.

Individuals who shift from always looking out for themselves to devoting time each week to conscientiously doing some good deeds for others have been positively changed. Those who may not have any scheduled plans to serve others but wait for direction from God every moment, and obediently and passionately accommodate His will as the day progresses, have made significant progress down the transformational pathway.

Spiritual transformation affords us the chance to relate to God in the most robust manner possible. Fully engaging in the transformation process redefines our self-image and life goals by establishing a renewed meaning and purpose to our existence, as well as modifying how we achieve fulfillment. It is, in current terms, an extreme spiritual makeover.

God wants you to be transformed. He doesn't discourage or prevent you from experiencing less substantial, positive changes, but

He never suggests that those minor alterations are the whole deal. In fact, sometimes it takes an accumulation of such changes to produce transformation.

But make no mistake about it, His goal for your life is that you cease to live for yourself. His best offer is for you to choose to live solely for Him, in which case He will guide your development in ways that maximize your potential. He wants you to define success according to your obedience to His will and pursuit of His vision for your life, rather than simply meeting the standards of the world — even the church world. His desire is for you to fill your mind and heart with thoughts about Him and for Him, instead of being consumed with the worldly options that are so readily available and enticing.

You have learned by now that the quality of your life is directly related to the choices you make. Every choice has consequences. For whom will you live: yourself or God? On whom you will be dependent for wisdom, power and resources: yourself or God? These are turning point decisions you must make in your life. You will experience the ultimate fulfillment in life by handing your life over to Him, and enabling Him to do unexpected, even supernatural things through you. In short, He wants you to be a twenty-first-century Jesus Christ as demonstrated by the holistic, seismic reshaping of why and how you live.

Oh, by the way, this is not an alternative to be accepted with remorse. I found that many people who consistently attend church, pray, volunteer and so forth — "good Christians" — secretly believe that handing the keys to God will result in a less exciting, less satisfying life. But my interviews with those who had followed through on God's plan energetically endorsed the transformed life as the only way to go.

GOD ALONE PROVIDES PURPOSE

More than 100 million American adults who describe themselves as Christian contend that despite their commitment to God they are still searching for clarity regarding their purpose in life. Tens of millions of self-described Christians feel unfulfilled in life, admit they lack direction, are disappointed that their faith has not produced the kind of meaning and identity they need, and question whether their life makes a difference. When you put it all together the picture describes a nation of individuals who are valiantly but unsuccessfully seeking to make sense of life and leave their mark on the world, but have not felt that their faith is helping them to reach their goals.

You've undoubtedly read the statistics showing that people who accumulate money, fame, material possessions and popularity admit that those achievements are not completely satisfying — something is still missing. That something, of course, is a deep connection with the Father who brought them into this world, wants to spend eternity with them, and has a phenomenal life in store for them — if they will just trust Him enough to work with His plan.

The only way to satisfy our impulse to thrive is to partner with God. He alone provides true meaning and purpose to our lives, and He alone is capable of multiplying our abilities to leave a lasting impression and have a renewing presence upon the world. To rise to our potential and make the most of life we have to get beyond ourselves and even transcend our natural limitations by cooperating with the God who wants to take us to places we cannot reach based on our own intellect and strength.

Think about it. America has more than 310 million people. Millions of them are smart — much smarter than you or me. Yet, millions of brilliant people doing their best work for decades and decades have failed to solve America's problems. Champions of moral living have failed to improve the ethical standards of our nation. Leaders in the religious world have failed to bring renewal to the hearts of our citizens. Why? Because based on our own talent and efforts, we are incapable of rising to the challenges we face.

Our only hope is for each of us to admit our limitations, recognize the incredible offer God has made to us, and keep Him waiting no longer. It is time for us — for you and me and every person who believes in God and the narrative provided in the Bible — to allow God to work through us in ways that bring lasting solutions, His solutions, to our lives individually and through us to this complicated and hurting world.

Your frustrations with life — concerning impact, purpose, identity, connectedness, image, reputation, joy, and security — are likely to diminish in direct proportion to the degree of God-centered transformation you experience. Ultimately, the key to the fulfilled life is to allow the loving, powerful Creator of all things to partner with you toward bringing about transformation. God is capable of doing it. He tells us that He is eager to do it.

That may be the least understood principle of the kingdom of God.

COMMITTING TO TRANSFORMATION

When you initially embraced Jesus Christ as your Lord and savior, you were undoubtedly told that this was the "good news." And, indeed it was, and is. But there's even more to the good news report: if you have accepted Him as your Heavenly Father and source of salvation, that's just the beginning of the journey. God is not done with you yet; there is more to this relationship than extracting eternal security!

If you are willing to cooperate with Him He still wants to fulfill His original dream for your life. That dream includes plans for a compelling life purpose, a continual sense of joy and peace, an intimate relationship with Him, a mind filled with timeless wisdom, a heart overflowing with love, a radical reduction of stress in your life, and more.

If you're like me, you read that list and think, "I'm okay with that..."

Those outcomes would be the result of your partnership with God in pursuing your complete spiritual transformation. To date you have experienced a portion — probably just a small portion — of the reconstruction He has in mind for you. Sadly, few American Christians ever experience the totality of what He has to offer. It's not His fault: few of us make the commitment and are sufficiently diligent to exploit His desire to make you a person whose character, decision-making, values and lifestyle are reminiscent of Jesus Christ.

If this sounds like a far-fetched reality, consider that there are countless historical examples of people whose lives have been re-sculpted by God to have unusual depth, fulfillment and influence, ranging from the Jewish patriarch Abraham and Israel's King David to the apostles Paul and Peter. Of course, millions of other Christ-followers throughout history have experienced the same kind of transformation, some of whom obtained timeless notoriety (Thomas More, Teresa of Avila, Thomas Aquinas, Saint John of the Cross, etc.) and others of whom lived in obscurity. You may even know some people who have reached the pinnacle.

I have spent the past six years studying the transformation process through various forms of qualitative and quantitative research, as well as Bible study and theological exploration. I do not pretend to com-pletely understand it. But I believe I have learned some things about this process that may help you to become the person God envisions.

We often think of transformation as a specific outcome, but it is more accurate to perceive it as a lifelong journey. Even our best ef-forts will result in an incomplete product for we are not fully trans-formed until we pass from this life to the next. In your remaining time on earth you have a chance to transition to a closer approximation of Jesus Himself — a much closer approximation. It is your opportunity to shift from living a life designed to succeed on earth to a life in which success is about the depth of your relationship with and service to God and His creation.

God will never force you to be transformed. It is your choice to move forward or stand pat. The opportunity to advance on the path to wholeness is available to every human being. God does not dis-criminate at all. He created you because He loves you and wants to nurture and cultivate that love to the fullest degree. But willingness and commitment are two very different realities. Simply making yourself available is necessary but insufficient to produce optimal results. God leaves the decision about how far you will go down the path in your hands.

Keep in mind that transformation does not happen because of your effort alone. When it takes place, transformation happens because you recognize that no matter how smart you are, how badly you want it, regardless of who you know, how churchy you have been, or how hard you try, you cannot become the godly person your heavenly Father meant you to be based solely on what you bring to the table.

Millions of people misunderstand what it takes to be transformed. It is common to mistakenly assume that possessing appropriate beliefs or engaging in laudable actions constitutes evidence of transformation. But you cannot become transformed solely (or mostly) by being active in a church or participating in a litany of religious rituals. Memorizing the entire Bible would be impressive and might be helpful, but by itself that will not transform you. There are various elements involved in the process — different practices, people, experiences, knowledge, commitments — but true spiritual transformation is impossible unless you become fully dependent upon God. Fully dependent. No human being is capable of producing spiritual transformation in their own life. God must pilot and control the process. Your job is to want this so badly that you become determined to cooperate fully with Him.

Let's find out how that kind of dependence really works.

CHAPTER 2

MAPPING THE JOURNEY

E veryone loves an extended vacation. Suppose you earned a two-week getaway after months of hard work. On the day you are scheduled to begin that time off, would you wake up that morning and ask yourself what you should do for the next two weeks? Of course not! You would have spent many hours over the previous months thinking about what you would most want to do, how to save up the money to do it, exploring your options, and developing a day-by-day plan for those two weeks.

On that first morning, then, knowing that you need to travel to your vacation destination, would you simply put your suitcase in your car and start driving, hoping that you will eventually find that destination if you drive earnestly and safely? Certainly not! You'd get directions and plan the drive accordingly. Maybe you'd print out directions from MapQuest or Google Maps, or perhaps rely upon a GPS system to guide you. If you're old school, you might get a map out of the glove compartment and carefully chart your route. Perhaps you'd even rely upon a driving plan and flip map you picked up at the automobile association. Whatever your preference, only a fool would simply turn on the car and randomly drive in the hope of reaching the desired destination.

That's how we treat our vacations — as if they are sacred escapes into personal renewal. But what about our spiritual renewal and development? Do we invest the same level of energy in meticulous planning and execution? Are we as careful about how we allocate our precious resources?

Unfortunately, after surveying the spiritual journey of several thousand people, it seems that we are pretty random about our efforts to experience genuine God-driven transformation. Think of it as a mindless mutiny: we refuse to give God control of our lives, but we're not really guiding the ship toward a particular destination that reflects our ultimate best interests; we just keep meandering in the ocean of life hoping to find an appealing place to dock. Forgive the impertinence, but sometimes it seems as if the Church — the aggregate collection of Christ believers — is indeed a ship of fools. We are not so much Christ followers as we are Christ admirers who listen to stories about His life and His teachings, then go about our business with a smile and a lobotomy.

What we need, then, is a map to help us figure out where we're going with our lives. Vacations are not the only life adventure we study and plan for; we strategically plot all kinds of things in our lives — the things that really matter to us, the aspects of life where we have little margin for error or desperately want to get it right. For example we plan our children's higher education, studying numerous college brochures, making visits to the campus, speaking to past and current students and staff before sending our child — and that check for tuition, room, and board — into a multi-year commitment with long-term implications. We plan our housing trajectory, typically getting married and living with parents or in an apartment before saving up enough money and getting sufficiently established in an area to buy a "starter house" and eventually upgrading to a larger, more comfortable home. Many families even map out their family meals, a practice that allows them to save time and money by purchasing food for multiple meals at a time when they go grocery shopping. Planning helps our life become more pleasant and productive.

We may treat the journey to wholeness in the same manner. Based on the research, we can now identify the stops on our lifelong adventure with God — not as a straitjacket that God must honor, or to preclude the mystery of how He works in our lives, but as a reasonable guide to help us stay focused and advancing. I will explain some of the exceptions and caveats later, but first let's identify each of the stops on our road to richness and develop a basic understanding of what each stop entails and how the entire journey unfolds.

THE TEN STOPS

Everyone's life starts out at the same stop on the journey. What happens after that is completely up to us. But the research indicates that the ultimate journey may take us from the beginning through a total of ten stops on our adventure toward maturity in Christ.

Here is a tour of the ten stops on the journey to wholeness.

STOP 1: IGNORANCE OF THE CONCEPT OR EXISTENCE OF SIN

When we are born, we have no tangible knowledge of the spiritual war between God and Satan, much less the choices we must make in the midst of the battle. Millions of people grow up oblivious to the fact that God exists and that He has provided moral and spiritual standards for us to satisfy. Others have some type of belief in God but are unaware of the concept of sin and how it relates to their reality.

The idea that they are sinners or commit sins does not register at any conscious level. Few Americans remain in this state of ignorance beyond their elementary school years.

Current population size: 1 percent of adults.

STOP 2: AWARE OF AND INDIFFERENT TO SIN

As life goes on, most people gain exposure to the idea of sin. That doesn't mean they believe it is real. (After all, to accept the idea of sin,

17

there must be a standard that defines sinful behavior or a holy being against which our behavior can be compared.)

This stop is populated by people who are intellectually aware of the meaning or concept but do not accept it as valid or significant. They may even understand the concept well enough to identify some of their own thoughts, words, and actions as meeting a particular definition of sin, but they remain oblivious because they reject the legitimacy of sin as a standard. They are not concerned about sinning; they are simply attuned to the fact that certain behaviors may be categorized as sinful. They may be aware that certain people believe sin is bad and has negative personal and cultural implications, but they remain disconnected from any meaningful concern about it.

Current population size: 16 percent of adults.

STOP 3: CONCERNED ABOUT THE IMPLICATIONS OF PERSONAL SIN

Moving beyond mere awareness of the concept of sin, people that reach Stop 3 begin to feel uneasy about the "what if" possibilities — as in "what if sin does offend God and it impacts my quality of life?" Or "what if my Christian friends are right — there is a God, sin ticks Him off, and I could spend the rest of eternity in Hell because of it?"

Motivated by such fears and concerns, these people begin to explore the implications of the various responses they could implement regarding sin. They could ignore it (i.e., it's unavoidable, or it's so common as to be meaningless, or it doesn't matter as long as you get away with it, or there is no ultimate penalty); continue to study the matter and try to understand the implications more fully; reduce their commission of sin so it is not as significant an issue; do a better job of hiding their sins from public view; or seek some way to wipe out their sins. The data indicate that most of the people at Stop 3 have some regular connection to a Christian church.

Current population size: 39 percent of adults.

STOP 4: CONFESS SINS AND ASK JESUS CHRIST TO BE THEIR SAVIOR

Fully apprised of the spiritual implications of sinning against God, and after a consideration of the options they may choose from, some people decide it is best to ask God for forgiveness and for Jesus Christ to save them from the eternal consequences of their sins. This most frequently happens in the presence of other believers, during which time the person seeking God's grace repeats some type of prayer or statement to invite Jesus into their life and save them from the condemnation that results from the failure to repent.

Subsequent to the profession of faith, people's next stop on the journey depends on what precipitated their immersion into the salvation experience at Stop 4. Because the journey is not always a progressive, linear adventure, some people will treat this as the pinnacle of their spiritual life and plateau here, continuing with the same level of religious activity and spiritual depth as they had prior to their salvation experience. Some will figure it's a "one and done" moment: "I said the prayer, I got the gift; now, where was I before this unexpected life interruption occurred?" Others will see Stop 4 as a point of departure into a different kind of spiritual experience and seek to go deeper with Christ. (We'll look at common paths taken after these descriptions.)

Current population size: 9 percent of adults.

STOP 5: COMMITMENT TO FAITH ACTIVITIES

The most common reaction after embracing Christ is to become more active in both personal spiritual growth and in a community of faith. The former enables the "new believer" to develop a more sophisticated understanding of the biblical narrative and its implications, often through educational forums such as Sunday school classes, Bible studies, and other Christian education courses. In addition, there is an expectation of personal investment in private growth efforts, such as "quiet times," Bible reading, scripture memorization, and embracing opportunities for service.

The latter reaction — participating in a community of believers — satisfies the need for belonging, which helps reform the new believer's self-image as a "new creation in Christ" and recognize his/her standing as part of a new, spiritual family. This often occurs through small groups that meet mid-week in people's homes to worship, study and pray together.

Current population size: 24 percent of adults.

STOP 6: EXPERIENCE A PROLONGED PERIOD OF SPIRITUAL DISCONTENT

After years of involvement in the Christian faith, most people slip into a spiritual coma. Their faith becomes a series of rituals, routines, recitations, rules, relationships, and responsibilities. Without noticing it, their spiritual goals also slip into a more relaxed state such that they are no longer stretching their faith muscles and pushing themselves to explore and master new spiritual territory. Rather than sustaining their passion for getting closer to God, they become comfortable with their spiritual experience.

But some people realize that there is a silent, unobtrusive kind of nagging that is troubling them regarding their faith. Those who explore the genesis of this inner turmoil sometimes conclude that it is because they have become spiritually numb, engaging in a religious life on auto pilot, and are missing the full relationship and life adventure with Christ that is available to them. This season of "holy discontent" — most likely instigated by God to jar them into re-evaluating what they want from Him and from life — is a major decision point for the believers who get this far along the journey. It is at this point in their pilgrimage that they must make some momentous choices.

They are often bored with local church activities: what should they do about their involvement at a local church?

They have discovered biblical reasons to question the validity of the local church system: should they continue to support it or seek an alternative?

They are painfully aware that their personal spiritual growth has plateaued: what must they do to reinvigorate their spiritual life?

The teaching and challenges they have received for the past few years have been lightweight and repetitive: is there greater depth to the Christian life, and how can they pursue it?

They have become tired of the pettiness, the politics and the meaninglessness of the relationships in their primary faith community: is the organized church a help or hindrance to a genuine Christian life, and how does one find or initiate a more appropriate community?

The disorganized missions trips and community service projects they experience cannot be the best option for using their gifts in service to others: how would Jesus have them invest their life in meaningful transformational activity?

This is a time when serious believers ask the right questions out of spiritual hunger, but are also susceptible to cynicism, doubt and frustration. Asking the right questions and getting the right answers are two different things.

Most believers who get to Stop 6 abandon the investigation once they realize the commitment and cost of moving forward on the journey to wholeness. Instead, they retreat to an earlier stop on the path and simply settle for what the local church and other spiritual entities have to offer. In the process they retain their good intentions but typically become either invisible or institutional "pillars." In other words, rather than pay the price of a deeper relationship with God, they retreat to the shelter of the religious games that ensnare most churched people.

A small proportion decides to grit it out, rejecting the "normal" Christian experience based on the trust that God has something more fulfilling in store for them if they will commit to completing the arduous journey. They cautiously decide to pursue a more challenging, all-encompassing, holistic faith experience. They are not sure what they are signing on for, but they figure it must be better than what they are presently enduring. The emphasis during this phase reflects the initial stages of integration — the blending and balancing of heart, mind, action and spirit.

Current population size: 6 percent of adults.

STOP 7: EXPERIENCING PERSONAL BROKENNESS

As believers dive into this new commitment, God meets them head-on with the realization that they are still too self-reliant and have never fully come to grips with the implications of their sin. Confession is one thing; feeling and dealing with the weight of what the confessed sins have done to their relationship with a holy and loving God is another. Some people have experienced a degree of brokenness, addressing their sin but not their independence, so God endeavors to show them the ravages of self-reliance.

So God takes them through a time of in-your-face confrontation. Serious believers finally reach a state of brokenness, which prepares them for the glorious healing and reconstruction that God has in mind for them. This takes them beyond merely accepting the offer of salvation to the experience of authentic, shared love and a truly purposeful life. But this brokenness only comes after much reflection and meditation, sorrow and remorse, realistic self-evaluation, talking and listening to God, and coming to the end of self as the "go to" person in all situations. This phase is largely about realigning our spirit with God's.

Current population size: 3 percent of adults.

STOP 8: CHOOSING TO SURRENDER AND SUBMIT FULLY TO GOD: RADICAL DEPENDENCE

God never wants us to remain shattered; His ultimate desire is for us to become one with Him and mature into the human beings He envisioned. But getting there is a difficult journey in and of itself.

The realization and understanding of our dilemma, which gets activated at Stop 7, merely sets us up for the major transition we go through at Stop 8.

It is at this juncture that we understand what total surrender, complete submission, and utter dependence upon God really mean. These are no longer concepts preached about or written about in a vague, arms-length manner; they now become the core of our existence.

To develop the maturity and the connection desired, we allow God to remake our life. Our normal pace slows down: mere activity is no longer as satisfying or meaningful because we have adopted a different goal. Silence, stillness, and solitude are built into our schedule to protect us from the distractions that have distorted our life and perspectives for so long. We begin every day consciously renewing our commitment to God, to trusting and following Him throughout the day. That produces an ever-present God-consciousness that changes our emotions, thoughts and deeds. We not only agree to give up control, but we actually do so; we do not act or speak until we sense direction from Him. We commit to seeing the world through God's eyes — and responding as we believe He would. We humble ourselves before God, but also gratefully accept spiritual guidance from other mature believers who are on the same journey. The alterations that occur at this stop on the journey are holistic and radical.

Current population size: 1 percent of adults.

STOP 9: ENJOYING A PROFOUND INTIMACY WITH AND LOVE FOR GOD

At some mystical point, God blesses us with the ability to know and love Him so profoundly that it is difficult to put into words. Reaching this point transforms everything. The believer experiences levels of joy, peace and wisdom previously unknown. Involvement in a faith community takes on a new meaning and investment in that community looks very different. Life assumes a new depth of purpose. Self-examination occurs with a different lens. Life is appreciated as a gift in strikingly divergent ways. Waking up every morning is suddenly more satisfying and exhilarating. Being a new creation in Christ has meaning that never could have previously understood or appreciated.

Current population size: 0.5 percent of adults.

STOP 10: EXPERIENCING A PROFOUND COMPASSION AND LOVE FOR HUMANITY

With their profound love of God in place, believers become able to see people the way God does and to love them as He loves them. The transformed believer engages with the world from a very different perspective and shares the joys and heartaches felt by God. Being the blessing to others that God made them to be consumes their hours. This is the ultimate life.

Current population size: 0.5 percent of adults.

THE RESEARCH BEHIND THE TEN STOPS

Now let's take a look at the distribution of people across the ten stops on the journey.

Let's focus for a moment on the numbers of people who park at any given stop of the journey. (See Table 1.) As we do so, please understand that these figures are not to be used in judgment against people. At best, these statistics are estimates based on primitive measures (self-report in surveys). Only God knows who is truly transformed and only He is qualified to judge anyone. Everyone is on the journey; some are early adopters, some are late bloomers, some are DOA, but you need not fret or gloat about how others are doing; like the man with the plank in his eye worried about the speck in someone else's, you have plenty to work through on your journey. These outcomes are displayed to help you assess your progress and hopefully to assist you in moving forward to the place that God yearns for us to reach (Stops 9 and 10).

Table 1
Distribution of Adults along the Transformational Journey

Stop 1: Unaware of sin	1%
Stop 2: Indifferent to sin	16%
Stop 3: Worried about sin	39%
Stop 4: Forgiven for sin	9%
Stop 5: Forgiven and active	24%
Stop 6: Holy discontent	6%
Stop 7: Broken by God	3%
Stop 8: Surrender and submission	1%
Stop 9: Profound love of God	0.5%
Stop 10: Profound love of people	0.5%

The most dramatic conclusion to draw from this information is that most of the people who ever pray to God to receive His forgiveness for their sins and to invite Jesus Christ to save them will probably never experience brokenness over those sins. Sadly, without that personal devastation, they cannot advance to the more significant places on the trail — or have the most fulfilling life possible.

As you can see, only one out of every twenty adults (about 5 percent) reaches the stage (Stop 7 and beyond) where their brokenness frees them from the crushing grip of sin and self. And it helps to explain why a mere 2 percent have fully surrendered their life and submitted it to God, or why just 1 percent have experienced the profound love connection that God yearns to have with us (Stop 9). (Note: To understand these statistics, realize that Stops 4 through 10 are not exclusive: some of the numbers must be combined to get a true picture. For instance, although Stop 4 is where people accept Christ as their savior, everyone from Stops 4 through 10 is born again. Everyone from Stops 7 through 10 has been broken. Everyone on Stops 8 through 10 have surrendered to God and submitted to His will.)

The table also shows another important insight. Of all the adults who make a profession of faith in Christ — that is, they become "born again" — there is surprisingly little to show for the effort. On numerous occasions Jesus talked about the fact that you can tell Christians by the spiritual fruit they bear, but the data suggest that just one out of every ten adults who accept Jesus as their Savior make any substantial changes in their spiritual routines and commitments.

Stated differently, a number of national studies I have conducted about people's views of their faith journey have indicated that most born-again Americans consider the assurance of their salvation through their profession of faith to be the end point of the journey. Nothing could be further from the truth.

Just as college graduation ceremony is called commencement, indicating the true beginning of the young adult's life, so does that acceptance of the free gift of God's grace mark the initiation of a more significant relationship and related experience with God. That gift was given because God wants a lasting and profound relationship with us. To deepen that connection requires the Christ follower to intentionally and purposefully pursue transformation. Receiving God's gift of forgiveness is simply the starting point of a more serious spiritual adventure.

STARTING WITH OURSELVES

If you look at the numbers in Table 1 and wonder what you can do to guarantee that the tens of millions of Americans double- and triple-parked at one of the first three stops on the journey to keep moving until they reach the final destination point, the answer is simple: nothing.

That answer seems so defeatist, so un-American, so unbiblical. But the truth is that only God transforms people, and He only transforms those who choose to cooperate with Him in the process. He will never force transformation upon someone. Just like someone's decision to seek salvation through God's forgiveness, transformation is a gift that God grants to those who desire it badly enough to abandon the world and pursue the kingdom. It is not a redefinition of character that He imposes upon those who are not sold out to the idea.

However, if you would like to influence someone to move toward such cooperation, perhaps your best strategy is to invest heavily in advancing your own spiritual development and depth, which will enable you to express the kind of selfless, surpassing love that is the heartbeat of Stops 9 and 10 of the journey. That is not all you can do, but it is certainly the best you can do. When you achieve that level of maturity you will have an undeniable influence on the world by virtue of who you have become — a Christ-like presence. Your impact on lives will be fueled by the power of God working through you in unique and unfettered ways. Yes, you can pray for the transformation of others, but it is better that we adhere to the principle in Matthew 7:3-5: clean up our own mess before we advise others how to clean up theirs. [5]

MARKETING SALVATION

A critical discovery of this project has been the mistaken understanding that tens of millions of people have about the idea of salvation. I think that the misconception is largely attributable to marketing. Please know that I have no qualms with the concept of marketing: it is simply an exchange of goods. The practice of marketing, in itself, has no moral content; the marketer supplies whatever moral or immoral underpinnings are related to the transaction. With that in mind, then, I'd suggest that we have mis-marketed salvation to the detriment of the kingdom of God, the Church, and the lives of millions of people.

To understand my concern, think about how a person "comes to Christ" in our society. The gift of God's grace, delivered through the sacrificial death and victorious resurrection of Jesus Christ, is often portrayed as the "free gift of salvation." Yes, it is free in the sense that you cannot buy it or earn it, but it is not "free" in the sense of it being given without any related responsibilities or expectations. Indeed, true salvation only comes when we are so heartbroken over the fact that our shameful treatment of God (i.e., through our sins) necessitated Jesus Christ's earthly presence, painful and unjust death, and miraculous resurrection that we then realign our lives, placing God in total control and adopting a wholly different set of values and life goals.

What most Americans consider their moment of "getting saved" is little more than a striking realization that they have sinned against a holy God who loves them deeply, wants "a relationship" with them, and has provided a way to compensate for their inappropriate behavior. And that's when marketing enters the picture. We are typically so eager to ring up another soul for the kingdom — or all too often for our personal reputation or our church's growth — that we condense the truth about the exchange in order to close the deal. Salvation becomes just another product to be sold to consumers. When the sale is successfully consummated we score another victory for the evangelist, the local church, and the kingdom of God.

Harsh words? Well, consider the way we have dumbed down the provision of God's grace. We tell the sinner his punishment is to suffer eternally in Hell. But fortunately there is one way, and only one way, out of the dilemma: God is offering the free gift — a kind of "get out of jail free" card — if you simply admit that you're not perfect, say you're sorry, and ask for His forgiveness. In exchange for that admission, you get a clean slate with God; in response to that request you receive God's promise of eternal life in paradise. There is usually no mention of accountability or on-going responsibility; this is a once-and-for-all solution to your sin problem. If you pray now, then God is obligated to give you the keys to the kingdom. Having studied these pitches in churches and evangelistic events around the nation, I have discovered that it is rare that such appeals include any mention of the need for brokenness, total dependence upon God, sacrificial living and servanthood, and the bearing of spiritual fruit as a sign of true renewal.

What we get, then, are millions of people who cannot resist the ultimate deal — a desirable product that's free, with no strings attached, minimal related expectations, and a lifetime guarantee. The most common expectations mentioned have to do with attending a church (which is not a biblical requirement) and living a good life (which we are incapable of doing without God's empowerment).

The research suggests — and your personal experience probably confirms — that few Christ-followers are so overwhelmed by the reality of their sin and the hopelessness of their life without God's grace that they are willing to beg Jesus for forgiveness and turn their life over to Him. That would represent a move toward brokenness and surrender. Sadly, the most common experience is for the one seeking the gift of grace to exhibit joy over getting the gift without having to give up anything significant (such as control of their life) or make any enduring commitments in return.

So we now have a nation of more than 100 million "born-again Christians" — based on those who have said some form of a "sinner's prayer" and invited Jesus to save them. Don't you think a country with 100,000,000 people who are sold out to Christ would be a country that reflects biblical standards and lifestyles? Wouldn't you expect a culture that is bonded to the heart of God to lead the rest of the world to the foot of the cross, by example even more than through words and religious events?

The relative unimportance of God's gift in the scope of their life is reflected by the fact that so few "saved" Americans bother to share Christ with nonbelievers; worship God every day in significant ways; work tirelessly at changing their life to avoid sinful opportunities and impulses; and redefine their self-image to see themselves as followers of Christ first and foremost. My research shows that most Americans who confess their sins to God and ask Christ to be their savior — i.e., "born-again Christians" — live almost indistinguishably from unrepentant sinners, and their lives bear little, if any, fruit for the kingdom of God.

Transformation is about more than winning the attendance pin at church, owning the latest and greatest "study Bible," donating more money to church than your neighbor, or fervently praying to God whenever you are in a bind. God's offer is to transform you into an imitation of Jesus Christ: a humble servant knowledgeable of and committed to God's will for your life. His design for your life represents a complete spiritual makeover, not a modest upgrade. And throughout the Bible He explicitly states that the evidence of being a true believer is the fruit that you produce for the kingdom of God. [6] In fact, Jesus harshly criticized followers who try to pass themselves off as disciples but whose lifestyle did not reflect transformation. [7] This may be the type of people Jesus was speaking about when He warned His disciples that many people would call Him by name, as if they knew Him, but that He would reject them as poseurs.

A LONG HARD JOURNEY

Do not be fooled into thinking that the transformational journey is necessarily a smooth, predictable, linear, or progressive adventure.

Many people are disappointed to discover that the journey is a fluid experience. For instance, after you make forward progress for a while you may well regress, returning to a less advanced point of maturity without any guarantee of eventually returning to a more advanced stop on the journey. Some people are confused when they experience persecution, pain, suffering, or condemnation — all of which are typically part of the process. Most believers are also stunned by how long and arduous the journey to wholeness is. And if you were hoping that the route to wholeness would be one of familiarity and serenity, think again. Every believer who doggedly pursues transformation with God will spend oodles of time outside of their comfort zone — emotionally, intellectually, spiritually, relationally, and behaviorally.

If you want to become the holy person whom God created you to be, prepare to pay the price. Jesus paid the most costly part. You must pay the most prolonged part. If ever there was a deal based on the "no pain, no gain" reality, this is it. That's a major reason why you will discover that the farther you go down the path of wholeness, the less company you'll have by your side. The traffic is thick and gnarled along the early stops of the journey; it thins out to almost nothing as you reach the end of the trail.

PATH 1: MOVING SEQUENTIALLY

So keep in mind that there are many different paths common to those who seek God's transformation for their life — not all of which please God. Naturally, the most common excursion — for the sake of identification, let's call it Path 1 — is to move sequentially down the road, from Stop 1 to whatever stop becomes the end point of the journey.

For those who take more circuitous or nonlinear paths, here are some of the most prevalent itineraries.

PATH 2: SETTLING FOR RELIGIOSITY

These people move from the starting line through the stops, eventually reaching Stop 6 (holy discontent). Their investigation of the options leads them to recognize that further growth will require them to experience brokenness. Rather than face that, they retreat to a life of comfortable and costless Christianity: attending church events, populating church programs, and doing some safe personal spiritual exercises. From that point forward most of them will never again move beyond Stop 5. Only a handful will eventually muster the courage and faith to let God take them through the stage of brokenness.

PATH 3: EXPLOITING CHEAP GRACE

This journey moves from Stop 1 through Stop 6. At that point, either burned out on church life, disappointed in the lack of spiritual depth experienced, or disinterested in investing more of themselves in the process, these people simply drop out of organized religion. They often figure they already got the best that Christianity had to offer — the "free gift of salvation" — and therefore focus their attention on other aspects of life. They revert from Stop 6 to Stop 2.

PATH 4: BECOMING ANGRY WITH GOD

This path is populated by people who went a stop further than those in Path 3. However, their experience at Stop 7 — brokenness — proved to be more than they were willing to endure, and they become angry with a supposedly loving and omnipotent Father who would subject them to such hardships. Sometimes this anger springs from an erroneous notion of what the Christian journey is designed to accomplish, and what we must experience to become our ultimate selves. Hurt by the experience of brokenness, these people turn their back on God and the Church, returning to Stop 2.

PATH 5: TRAVELING THE BIBLICAL PATH

This approach may be the most biblical of all. After reaching Stop 3 (concern over sin), these individuals leapfrog to Stop 7 and deal with the reality of their sin appropriately. Having experienced the brokenness that God seeks in us, they then ask for His forgiveness and grace before immersing themselves in various faith endeavors, surrendering their lives, and loving toward the end of the journey.

But these different pathways simply describe what other people do. You're not directly responsible for them, only for yourself. Take a few moments to reflect on where your heart, mind, strength and soul stand at this moment. Which path are you on? What stop of the journey are you at right now? Do you need to make any changes in your progression?

CHAPTER 3

THE NEED TO SELF-ASSESS AND ADJUST

A few years ago I coached my daughter's school basketball team. I will never be voted into the Coaches' Hall of Fame, but we had a winning season, a lot of fun, and learned some valuable lessons along the way. One of those lessons emerged from watching the coach of a team we were playing.

I approached the game aware that our opponent had several very talented players — I had watched them play on other teams around town. We would have to play effective defense to win. Our practices leading up to the game emphasized that strategy. The game itself, however, was a blowout; we won without having to stretch ourselves. Watching from the sidelines, I was amazed at how poorly organized and nonresponsive our opponent was — a failing I attributed to their coach. They seemed to freelance on every play, and showed little interest in playing defense. They played an undisciplined version of run-and-gun: shoot as often as possible and hope you can outscore your opponent without working up a sweat on defense.

At the final buzzer I strode down the sideline to shake hands with the coach and thank him for the game. I commented on how it must have been frustrating for him that his girls didn't seem to have followed any game plan or run their plays. He gave me a puzzled look and said he felt everything had gone pretty much as expected. He briefly noted that his "game plan" was for the girls to have fun and not get injured — that was the extent of his vision and preparation for the contest.

Walking away from that conversation I was reminded of something I'd learned in my three decades of survey research and implementation: you get what you measure.

The opposing coach believed that the purpose of the game was not to win but for the girls to have fun — as if those two ends were mutually exclusive. His metrics were pleasure and safety. Ours were victory, sportsmanship, teamwork, and personal excellence. The two teams shared the same court that day, but they did not share the same purposes.

The trajectory of your relationship with God depends on your metrics: what is your goal? That, as much as anything else, determines which transformational pathway you will follow, and how far you will get on the journey. If you don't care much about God or eternity, you're not likely to get very far; your metrics will examine personal happiness, lifestyle comfort, wealth accumulation, and personal health. If, however, you live for God, then you will use a completely different set of measures — ones designed to help you keep moving toward a more Christ-like life and more spiritually fruitful journey.

To effectively measure your progress, there are various scriptural benchmarks you might examine en route to wholeness. In other words, it is practically impossible to become the person God intends you to become unless you can answer the basic question: transformed into what?

What are you being transformed into? Is it sufficiently God-honoring to acknowledge your sinfulness or do you also need to be the best church member, parent, spouse, employee, and citizen you can be? Is being a born-again Christian sufficient to get you through life, or is there more to the journey than gladly taking salvation from God and then continuing to live as if nothing had changed? How much is enough? Can a Christian reach a place on the journey and simply give up the battle, believing that he has done enough to please God?

AN "IMPOSSIBLE" LIST

Genuine transformation is about becoming something more than a good person, an exemplary church member, or a productive citizen. Those could be indications of transformation in progress, but they are not the final goal of the process. As you ponder the question of what you are being transformed into, consider the following possibilities prescribed by the scriptures.

Jesus spoke frequently and passionately about the kind of people we are to become and those themes were repeated and amplified by the other authors of New Testament texts (Luke, Paul, James, John and Peter). Based on Jesus's words we can see that we are meant to be transformed into people who are:

Trustworthy servants [8]	Merciful
Followers of Christ	Paragons of integrity
Obedient, holy	Prayer warriors
Lovers of people	Pursuers of God's will
Lovers of God	Supporters of the needy
Evangelizers	Repentant sinners
Peacemakers	Grateful receivers of God's gifts
People of abundant faith	Generous stewards
Fearless believers	Morally blameless and alert
Students of scripture	At peace with life
Passionate worshipers of God	Joyful
Humble	Friends of Christ
Role models	Persecuted believers
Forgiving	Lovers of truth
Seekers of justice	

My first reactions to that list were *That's impossible*, and *Just reading that list makes me feel tired.* Is it even vaguely possible that you could become this kind of person without giving up control of your life and allowing the power of God to bring about such a transformation? Absolutely not! As the Bible reminds us, nothing is impossible for God — not even reshaping you and me into His image and restoring our mind, heart, body and soul for His glory.

MEASURING AMERICAN CHRISTIANS

So if God provides us with both the plan (in scripture) and the power (through the Holy Spirit) to become a fully transformed person, why then is it that more than 80 out of every 100 Americans call themselves Christian yet only 1 out of every 100 are broken, surrendered, submitted, and loving? And how do we really know, for that matter, just where any of the nearly 200 million self-proclaimed Christian adults in America stand on the journey?

Again, it all goes back to how and what you measure. If you think maximizing your faith simply demands an unblemished attendance record at worship services and Sunday school, then that's probably as far as you will go on the journey. But if you're ready and willing to do some deeper work to mature in your relationship with God — willing to pay the price and live to godly life — you're likely to develop some invaluable measures that will help keep you on the path toward holiness.

On the following pages are three data tables that reflect some of the measures used in my research to estimate where we, as a nation of professed Christ-followers, currently stand on the journey. You can shake your head at some of the statistics, but more importantly, look at your own life in relation to these measures and conduct an honest assessment of how you stack up on these indicators of the heart, mind, action, and spirit. Until you get real with yourself — and vulnerable to God — you probably won't get much farther along the journey. Your personal rebellion against the authority of God will continue to hinder your development into the person God made you to be.

36

Table 2
What Christians Think, Believe, and Feel
(Base: Self-described Christians, 18 or older)

10% have a biblical worldview

12% say that their reality of their sins has caused them to have an emotional crash

14% say their faith in God is their highest priority in life

15% say every moral choice they make is consistent with the Bible

16% believe that absolute moral truth exists and that it is defined by the Bible

17% say the Bible is the medium or resource that has the greatest influence on their decisions

19% say that they, as individuals — not government, businesses, churches, or non-profits — have the primary responsibility for addressing human poverty

24% consider themselves to be holy

30% have heard of the "spiritual gifts" and are able to identify one that they say they possess

36% say it is important to have active and healthy relationships with people who are not Christian

36% believe that success in this life is determined solely by their obedience to God

38% believe that God expects them to become holy

40% are struggling with stress and anxiety

41% believe that when Jesus Christ was on earth He sinned

49% say they are passionate about social justice

54% believe that doing your best to be obedient to biblical admonitions is what provides spiritual wholeness

58% believe that the Holy Spirit is a symbol of God's presence, power or purity, but is not a living or impactful entity

58% believe that if you are a good person, or do enough good things, they can earn their way into Heaven

59% believe that Satan, or the devil, is a symbol of evil but is not a living or impactful entity

Keep in mind that all of the statistics on the following pages are among those who call themselves "Christian."

RESEARCH REGARDING OUR MIND AND HEART

The research findings listed in Table 2 provide several helpful insights into our slowness at inviting God to join us on the journey.

First, we are stymied by unbiblical theology that distorts our understanding of God, life, how the world works, and the role of faith and spirituality in our decision-making. It becomes evident — not only from this research, but from other studies conducted, as well — that the influence of our postmodern culture on our beliefs about God, Jesus, the Bible, spiritual war, and other matters of faith is huge — and harmful.

Second, we see that American Christians are resilient. We maintain that we are strong enough to handle what the world throws at us — without the intervention or assistance of God. We tend to keep Him at bay, holding Him in our pocket as a secret weapon to call upon when things get really difficult. In general, we continue to view success by worldly standards — popularity, achievement, accumulation, comfort — and believe that truth is ours to determine. We might sometimes consult the Bible for guidance in such ruminations, but believe that determining right from wrong is ultimately up to us.

Third, the burden of playing God's role in our life gets heavier as the years progress. This burden also affects our identity and sense of holiness. Without the power of the Holy Spirit leading and supporting us, we seek to manage every aspect of each day using our native intelligence and intuition. The results of that strategy are obvious.

RESEARCH REGARDING OUR BEHAVIOR AND ACTIVITY

The data in Table 3 show where the rubber meets the road — the "fruit" that Jesus described as the only valid evidence that we have been transformed.

Table 3
What Christians Do—and Don't Do
(Base: Self-described Christians, 18 or older)

6%	tithed last year
11%	have a conversation about faith in a typical week with someone who believes differently than they do
16%	avoid conversations about faith out of fear of their spiritual ignorance being discovered
19%	engaged in a fast from food, for spiritual purposes, during the past three months
20%	contend that the most important decision they have ever made was to become a Christian
21%	say it is imperative for a person to be connected to a community of faith if they want to mature spiritually
22%	state that they are completely dependent upon God
29%	serve as a spiritual or moral mentor to someone on a weekly basis
29%	talked to someone who believes differently than them about faith matters in the past week
30%	tutored or befriended an underprivileged child in the past year
35%	provide moral or spiritual advice to people under age 17, other than their own children
35%	have made a verbal confession of their sins to another Christian within the past three months
40%	engaged in an intensive study of the Bible during the past three months
41%	visited an elderly or sick shut-in within the past year
42%	have had a time of extended spiritual reflection within the past three months
44%	had a prolonged time of focused prayer during the past three months
44%	said they would not change anything significant about their life
47%	donated some time to serve poor people in the community in the past year
56%	read the Bible, other than at church, during the past week
59%	say they practice daily worship
69%	attended a worship service during the past month, other than a special event such as a wedding or funeral service
98%	prayed to God in the past week

If anything, these numbers suggest that we have effectively com-partmentalized our faith. We do not give as generously as we could; we are not likely to talk about our faith except in safe environments; and we rarely engage in the traditional spiritual disciplines (e.g., fasting, contemplation, solitude). Our focus is more often inward than outward or upward.

Combined with the other studies I have conducted over the past three decades, what we witness is a body of Christians who are reactive more than proactive and reflective with their faith. Because the attitudes, beliefs and values listed in Table 2 are the fundamental drivers of our activity, the behaviors and inclinations displayed in the Table 3 are predictable, if generally disappointing. But they do indicate a group of people who are not prepared to move deeper into the transformed life.

RESEARCH REGARDING OUR FAITH AND SPIRITUALITY

As you consider the data in Table 4, several striking perspectives emerge. For instance, American Christians do not particularly cherish or pursue truth. We are quite blasé about allowing the Holy Spirit to show us the way forward or about making a total commitment to growing spiritually. No wonder so many Christians are uncertain about their life's purpose, fuzzy regarding their spiritual gifts, and wrestling with anxiety.

Our conversations with God, through prayer, are limited. We do not hear clearly from God very often, if at all; we are confused about His guidance as often as we are convinced. In fact, most Christians admit that God is not in their consciousness very often.

Overall, we place a relatively low value on our relationship with Christ as evidenced by how lowly we rank that connection and our decision to accept Him as our savior. We are inconsistent in our willingness to cooperate with God. That may be due to the widespread refusal to see life as a spiritual battle in which you take sides and live with the consequences of your choice.

Table 4
The Spiritual Side of American Christians
(Base: Self-described Christians, 18 or older)

18% claim they are totally committed to investing themselves in spiritually development

20% say the most important decision they have ever made was asking God for forgiveness and inviting Jesus to be their Lord and Savior

20% indicate they are making a full commitment to their spiritual development

23% claim the most important relationship in their life is with Jesus Christ or God

25% believe that God is always on their mind or in their consciousness

42% say they consistently cooperate with God to do what He wants

43% claim to be on a journey to discover and understand spiritual truth

44% are totally certain that Jesus speaks to them in personal and relevant ways

45% contend they feel a deep sorrow about their sins that has changed their thinking and behavior

52% believe there is a lot more to the Christian faith than they are currently experiencing

53% admit that they are still trying to figure out the meaning or purpose of their life

56% claim to regularly make time and expend effort to listen to God

56% say they consistently allow their life to be guided by the Holy Spirit

61% say they either side with God or with Satan — there is no in-between

The numbers contained in these three tables are not exactly the profile you'd expect for people whose life assignment is to imitate God, be holy, and serve as a light to the world. [9]

Not surprisingly, this state of affairs has crippled the Christian Church in this country. The behavior of alleged Christians has darkened the image of the Christian faith and diminished the influence of Christianity's role in our culture. It has left tens of millions of spiritually-inclined people dissatisfied with their personal faith experience, the depth of their moral wisdom and influence, and the value of their connection to the broader community of Christians and faith-based institutions. Things haven't worked out as expected.

An optimistic spin on these figures, though, is that the journey to wholeness remains available to everyone — even those who have been utterly complacent to this point — if they are simply willing to walk alongside Jesus. Imagine the difference it would make in individual lives as well as in American society if all who consider themselves to be Christ followers accepted God's invitation to pursue a fuller and more fulfilling life with Him. The world would be turned upside down.

* * * * *

But, of course, it's never easy. In the interest of full disclosure, let's briefly consider the price of the transformed life.

Growth always comes with a cost. Jesus warned His followers that the cost of discipleship was total commitment and surrender, proven by love. [10] Unfortunately, millions of Americans want to advance beyond what they are willing to commit to spiritually. Every attempt at reaching the next stop on the transformational journey comes with a price tag. Often, people reach for the next level and test it out, only to retreat once they discover the price — especially if pain or sacrifice is involved. They may hold off and then try again in the future, hoping they are capable of paying the price, but might retreat again if they discover that they still can't make the required investment. It is not uncommon for people who have been serious and intentional about realizing their transformational potential to abandon their pilgrimage because they refused to endure the suffering or hardship experienced at the next level, or to surrender whatever was required to elevate their relationship with God to a higher plane.

When people overstep their transformational threshold and return to the previous, more comfortable stop on the journey, they usually wind up settling for that place. After one or more failed attempts at maturing God's way, they cease pushing forward and accept their new comfort zone, sacrificing what could have been great for what is comfortable.

Why do people suffer defeat on the journey? Sometimes it is attributable to our failure to fully cooperate with Him or to effectively absorb some of the lessons provided at a particular stop on the journey. When we meet with such a setback, it is meant to be temporary, but many people accept it as a final outcome. (Remember, no pain, no gain.) By settling for less than we could have had in our relationship with God, we trade present relief and adequacy for potential ascendancy.

Lasting progress is realized only when we build upon the lessons learned earlier in the journey. The transformation process should not be thought of as linear and sequential. Perhaps because transformation occurs in the midst of spiritual war, our journey is in a constant state of turmoil, characterized by an ebb and flow of progress and regress. That is why there are such varied paths that people follow in their effort to reach the endpoint of the full journey. There is an efficient route (see Path 5 in chapter two), but some of us deviate from that ideal path and take detours. That doesn't mean we cannot finish the race well; it just means we may take longer to get there and expend more resources along the way.

Another complexity is that most Christ-followers focus upon allowing transformation to happen in one or two of their four life dimensions. As Jesus noted, your life is a complex blend of four dimensions — heart, mind, strength and soul. Accordingly, full transformation happens in relation to all four dimensions; God did not design you to be imbalanced and incomplete.

Your transformational journey is designed to affect your mind (what you think and believe, your worldview), your heart (what you feel and love, your intuition), your strength (your body and behavior), and your soul (your moral and spiritual commitments, connection with God and truth). In Mark 12:30-31, which Jesus identified as the greatest of the commandments, He indicated that we become transformed by loving God and people through all four dimensions. Most of us, though, are comfortable with one or two of those dimensions and tend to ignore the others. It is the decision to dismiss one or more dimensions that retards or even halts our spiritual maturation.

Transformation takes a long time. Once we commit to the process the timetable is determined by God, not us, although our proficiency at embodying the lessons of the journey affects that schedule. Regardless, the research suggests that this journey is a marathon, not a sprint; it takes decades, not mere months or years, and we never finish. If you are serious about transformation, settle in for the long haul. Becoming the person God wants you to be is a lifelong commitment.

OBSTACLES TO TRANSFORMATION

Because transformation God's way enables you to become the most complete person you could be, one must wonder why anyone would choose to not commit to the journey. The research revealed a parcel of reasons that keep people from seeking God's best for their lives.

One common reason, touched on earlier in this chapter, is that our standards for evaluation are different from God's. Have you ever caught yourself saying that you're not perfect but you're "better than most people"? We forget that God does not grade on a curve and fool ourselves into thinking that above average is good enough. That mentality reflects how lightly we treat God and His standards. We often attempt to satisfy personal benchmarks related to behaviors such as consistent attendance at church services, completion of personal Bible reading goals and number of hours volunteered to the ministry. These are not inherently bad, but they are far removed from the idea of having a profound intimacy with God and becoming a life-changing blessing to other people. Too easily we get caught up in chasing the superficial.

Another common reason for abandoning the transformation journey is pure ignorance. Shockingly few Christians have ever learned or thought about the concept and process of transformation. Many have been the victims of bad theological training, adopting the idea that having attained the promise of salvation is enough — their place in Heaven is supposedly "secure" — so they need not stretch beyond that. As a result they have no sense of urgency to pursue spiritual depth and no comprehension of the biblical standard that has been set for us. We get comfortable going with the flow and assume that if something is meant to be, God will facilitate it or it will happen naturally.

The research showed that some of the more committed or informed followers of Christ are aware of the transformational process, but it is simply too painful or intimidating for them to embrace. Granted, in a culture where spiritual breadth and tolerance transcends spiritual depth and absolutes, the building blocks of transformation are daunting; endeavors such as confession, surrender, service, brokenness, suffering, solitude, humility, daily worship, simplicity and silence are not popular ideals, even if they lead to growth. The all-too-frequent compromise position is to pick and choose aspects of the journey that are less rigorous or more palatable, and to focus on those to the exclusion of the more demanding or frightening aspects.

The evidence also shows that many devoted Christians work hard at creating a developmental routine but they lack any kind of accountability for transformation. [11] Because the rest of life does not stop as we pursue transformation — indeed, for it to be genuine transformation, it must happen in the context of our daily struggles and challenges — we get easily distracted and bumped off course. Without adequate support — people to check in on how we're doing, to either encourage us, give us ideas to consider, or to provide the "big boy" talks that snap us back in line — the journey becomes more meandering than we would ever have predicted.

Can you relate to any of these obstacles? Do some of these barriers describe your reluctance to becoming all that God intends for you? Take solace in the fact that you are not alone. But recognize these perspectives for what they are: a chasm between who you are and who you could be if you trusted God enough to let Him rule your life.

Contemporary society provides an enormous number of barriers along the path. Some are obvious: immoral or distracting media messages, consuming relationships, cultural obsessions such as wealth or status, education that instills errant values, inferior parenting, laws and public policies that permit unwarranted behavior. Other pitfalls are less obvious: unbiblical preaching, compromised church standards, the absence of mature spiritual mentors, robotic worship practices, superficial prayers, and the like. Transformation demands commitment and determination, as well as goals, measurement and accountability if serious progress is to be made.

SECTION 2

JENNIFER'S JOURNEY

CHAPTER 4

UNDERSTANDING THE FRUSTRATION

NOVEMBER 12, 10:37 P.M.

So, here I am, sitting in my living room, thinking. It's been nine years since I prayed to accept Jesus as my savior. What a ride it has been!

I can remember some things like they were yesterday. I need to recall them, because somehow they've led me to my current state of spiritual malaise. I'm stagnant, and it's getting worse.

All the things that used to pump me up have become boring and meaningless. Not that I am doubting Jesus is the way! But I feel surrounded by a hollow, superficial, cultural Christianity that makes me mad.

There must be more to the Christian life than this!!!

NOVEMBER 13, 4:14 P.M.

I remember the first conversation I had with Doug. He was a pretty cool youth pastor. He said that the only thing missing in my charmed life back then was Jesus. I had no idea what he was talking about. Actually, I remember thinking he had no idea what *he* was talking about! I *was* a Christian; I'd gone to church all my life!

But as he talked about the divide between me and God because of my sins, I sensed deep inside that he was right. I was really upset — not mad, just uncomfortable, maybe even disappointed with that realization. Later that night I called Doug and told him I needed to get right with God. He came over, we prayed, I cried, and I felt a strange, indescribable sense of happiness.

Remember that, Jen? Where did that go!?!

The first person I shared Christ with was Molly. She was in her hell-raising period and I was in my afterglow from accepting Jesus. I invited her to lunch. Let's see, where did we go? Oh yeah, the Bread Basket Cafe. I was being all symbolic — Jesus is the bread of life, etc. etc. Oh brother.

I remember we got into it pretty heavy. She was livid that I would "judge" her or "force" her to accept an answer to a problem she denied having! I was probably more self-righteous and insufferable than I'll ever know. But I didn't recognize it. I just felt bad that Molly might not go to heaven.

I didn't see much of Molly again. I still feel sad for her. I hope she has found the Lord.

Shortly after that, Doug and some of his friends — I remember Katy and Ashley but there may have been others — invited me to attend their church.

Boy, was First Baptist different from All Saints! What a shock the service was. No robes, no stained glass, no liturgy, no "passing of the peace," not even the hard pews! The sermon seemed endless — 45 minutes?! — but it also was more earnest than the homilies my old Episcopal priest used to read. Maybe that was because now I was more interested in the Bible.

Anyway, the thing I'll always remember most is how friendly the people were after the service. The church only had 150 people or so, but it seemed like every one of them came up to meet me. I suddenly felt like I belonged — as if I was part of a family, not just a "member" whose duty it was to be there every Sunday and drop money in the donation plate.

NOVEMBER 15, 6:14 P.M.

Still trying to remember everything...

Oh yeah, Dr. Osborne's Sunday school class. I learned so much! I was mesmerized by the biblical truths he taught — and amazed at how little I knew!

That 18-month series he led on developing a biblical worldview was really life-changing. Where had I parked my brain when I was at All Saints? Or hadn't they used scripture much?

What else? Let's see. Over the next five or so years I was so active in the church that I marvel at it now: Sunday services, Sunday school, small group, women's fellowship, prayer meetings, church-wide retreats, volunteer with the teen ministry, serving food once a month to the homeless, listening to the sermons (again) on CD (later on via podcasts — how things have changed!), becoming a deacon, driving to Mexico or to inner city locations over long weekends for missions trips, supporting our foreign missionaries... Where did I find the time to sleep, eat and hold down a job?!

Good memories. Lots of good friends and spiritual growth.

But now? What's happened to me?

NOVEMBER 16, 11:22 P.M.

These last three or four years — it seems that my faith has unraveled. Why? Nothing monumental has triggered this frustration. I'm healthy and have friends and have a good job, etc., etc. But everything seems so ... predictable. Flat. Where is Jesus?

The sermons all sound the same. A few basic concepts repackaged with a new story or two before we get a few superficial applications. The worship music sounds the same — upbeat and mindless. The educational programs don't dig deep. Our outreach efforts are pretty lame, which is probably why they appear to produce minimal results. And our service projects, while they're well-intended efforts at helping the poor, never really get to the root of the problems, so we have to keep doling out food, clothing, money, housing, and everything else.

But it's not just the church. My spiritual life is as empty as Jesus's tomb. (Ha, girl, aren't you clever!) But really!

Does God even hear me when I pray?

I haven't gotten anything new or stimulating out of the Bible in a while.

Giving to the church — why bother? It just goes to feed the beast, paying salaries and building expenses, but it's not really about life change, is it?

Even my spiritual conversations with Ami, Rashell, Donna, Kayla — my most devout friends! — seem trite and mandatory (because we're Christians "sisters").

And ultimately meaningless.

NOVEMBER 17, 12:15 A.M.

I've had "dry" spells in my spiritual walk before, but nothing like this. I'm so disappointed — in me, in the church. In God!

Please, Jesus, assure me that this is not all there is! You couldn't possibly have died and put this whole Christian thing together simply so that we would all arrive at this place. There must be more! Where's the deeper level, something really special that average people like me can tap into without having to join a convent or live in a monastery?

How do I get beyond the same old, same old?

Maybe I just need a plan. I suppose I could start by talking to people — safe people, which really narrows the possibilities — about my dilemma.

If this is as good as it gets, I either need to lower my standards and expectations, or else review my long-term commitment to Christianity. Is that an awful thing to say? Will I go to hell for even thinking that?

It's just that sometimes this voyage on the good ship Christ Imitator seems to have run aground, and I feel like I'm drowning in spiritual angst. I can't stand it any longer. Somebody throw me a spiritual life jacket!

WHY DID JESUS DIE FOR US?

Jennifer was frustrated, but she didn't allow herself to wallow for long. She knew she needed to reach out. She made a list of the brightest, most committed Christians she knew and could trust.

First on the list was Dr. Wilson Neilsen. Dr. Neilsen was a former pastor who had returned to his first love, teaching. He now taught religion courses at a community college. Jennifer recalled that while interacting with Dr. Neilsen when he still was her pastor, he seemed fair, open-minded and a deep thinker. He always reflected the serenity and love of Jesus with people he encountered — even church people who were ugly toward him when he announced he was leaving the church staff.

On the day of the visit, she felt a bit nervous, until Dr. Neilsen gave her a big hug. His office was lined with books. She sat in a comfy old chair facing his oak desk, and they chatted a bit about what they both had been doing since he left First Baptist. Then Jennifer took a big breath and began.

"So, Dr. Neilsen, what's my problem? Why has Christianity lost its magic for me? Is this a sign I'm going to hell?"

She laughed nervously while watching his face.

He smiled at her attempt at humor and took a couple of seconds before responding. "First, Jennifer, please call me Wil. I'm not big on formality. As to your problem, as you called it, I think this is one of the best things that could have happened to you. And it's a sign of God's love, not condemnation."

He noted her perplexed look. "In fact, if you didn't reach this point of confusion and uncertainty, a period of dissatisfaction with your religious activities — that would be cause for concern. All you've done is reach the end of your tolerance for religion."

Jennifer frowned. Was he taking this opportunity to launch into a diatribe about the superficiality of the church and strike back at those who had done him wrong?

He smiled. "Your soul is craving spiritual authenticity. How long has it been since you accepted Christ as your savior?"

Jennifer him it has been a bit more than nine years.

He nodded. "That's actually a bit quicker than many people reach the point of discouragement. But here's the thing — "

He leaned closer and his eyes glowed with intensity.

" — This is likely to be the most important time in your life. You asked Jesus into your heart. You've invested yourself in church life. You've put time into reading the Bible and praying. You've become part of the community of believers. All those things are good. But they're not the point. They're not what God has called you to."

Jennifer was beginning to feel uncomfortable.

"You see, so far your faith journey has been all about you. Satisfying your needs, answering questions, developing friendships, gaining security, learning religious information, being in the right places. None of that is bad, and it may even have been necessary for you to get to this point. But none of that is what Jesus died for.

"It's time for you to grow up, Jennifer."

MORE THAN BEING A GOOD CHRISTIAN

Jennifer was stung.

"But Dr. Neilsen — Wil — I've followed the path of every mature" — here she drew quote marks in the air — "Christian I know. I've done what my church asked of me. What else was I supposed to do?"

Wil maintained his intensity, and his eyes narrowed as he continued.

"Don't be offended, I'm not putting you down. I'm just offering an observation and a ray of hope. You see, contrary to popular perception — and church teaching — Jesus did not die simply for you to have a free pass to Heaven."

Wil paused to let that sink in. Then he continued. Jesus died because He wants His children's love, he said. Taking His free gift and giving Him cursory lip service does not constitute a relationship.

"Jesus's goal is to transform our lives," Wil said. "To move us from being a comfort-seeking, success-driven, religious, selfish sinner to a God-loving, God-fearing, God-focused, Spirit-led, heartbroken, citizen of Heaven."

Jennifer shot back that she had heard this all before.

"That's exactly why I did all the things you described before — attending church, reading the Bible, praying, serving the poor, giving money. I'd hardly call that lip service."

"But what was your motivation?" Wil asked, looking at her straight in the eye. "Did you do those things for Him, to get close to Him, or because that's what a good Christian does?"

Jennifer was silent. Wil got up and walked to his window. He gazed out for a moment before responding.

"Americans often misinterpret the meaning of salvation," he

continued, "thinking it is God showing His profound love for us, forgiving us, and accepting us. And indeed, that's part of it. But He offered His Son as an olive branch, not because He was in a position of weakness and needed to impress us or win us over.

"Jesus, the holy and almighty God in the flesh, died an ugly, unjust, painful death so that we would understand how serious He is about becoming intimate with you. He rearranged the laws of both the invisible and the material world for that to happen, as seen through the miracles and the resurrection.

"His ultimate hope is that each of us would want to know Him and love Him, and to do that at the deepest level. He wants to transform us from the worldly sinners we are to holy imitators of Jesus.

"Sadly," Wil continued, returning to his office chair, "Americans have made salvation the ultimate deal, a can't-lose transaction. We hear that God wants to give us the free gift of salvation and all we have to do is accept it, so we jump in. We love free stuff!"

Jennifer broke a smile, and Wil chuckled too.

"Yes, it's free in the sense that we cannot earn our way into God's eternal presence, but our part of the bargain is that when we say we're sorry for our offenses against God, we're supposed to mean it. We ought to have our hearts so shattered by our realization of our rottenness and His goodness that we commit to changing from A to Z — our purpose, values, behavior, standards, and goals. The whole enchilada," he said, smiling.

"And that's what the concept of transformation by God is about."

Jennifer was looking at the floor. She tilted her head, and looked up at Wil.

"What is this transformation you're talking about? Maybe I don't understand that."

He took a deep breath, smiled and came around to lean on the front of his desk. "And that's the right question! Not many people understand how salvation is just the beginning of the transformation process — the journey to wholeness!"

WHY ARE WE HERE?

The journey to wholeness.

Jennifer rolled that around her mind for a moment. She didn't want to say it to Wil, but the phrase sounded a bit cliché. Maybe even New Age-y. Everyone promised a journey to wholeness.

"I know what you're thinking," Wil said, startling her. "Our society promises wholeness all the time. And people are hungry for transformation, aren't they? Intellectual transformation through extended education; physical transformation through exercise, dieting and nutrition; even emotional transformation through marriage, parenting, and divorce. My question is, Why don't we take spiritual wholeness, spiritual transformation, as seriously? In fact — "

"But — " Jennifer jumped in. "Wil, isn't that what all the church activities and commitments to discipleship are all about? Transformation? And don't we do that only because we received salvation as God's gift through Jesus?"

"Really?" he asked with a grin. "When you go to a church service, for whose benefit do you worship?"

Jennifer thought for a moment and answered honestly. "Okay. For me. God doesn't need my worship. It is a demonstration of my submission and praise."

"Uh-huh," Wil grunted. "Does the Bible command us to worship God because it's good for us, or because God desires it?"

Jennifer's shoulders dropped. She knew Wil was going to shred her statement, and he did.

"You say God doesn't need our worship. Then why did He create us? Think about the first of the Ten Commandments. What's it about? The importance of us worshiping Him, and doing it with purity. The Psalms are all about how much God craves and enjoys our worship.

I'm sure you've heard preachers and worship leaders talk about the fact that 'God inhabits the praises of His people.' And didn't He instruct the Israelites to worship Him regularly because it showed they were serious about loving and obeying Him?"

"Okay, okay." Jennifer held up hands. She looked a little shaken. "I was really thinking of 'need' as if God is conceited and wants our flattery. I do understand that I was designed to praise Him."

"What else have you been taught is the reason for your life?"

Jennifer inwardly chafed at the set-up, but answered, warily. "There are many ways you can answer that, but I'd probably cite Mark 12, where Jesus talks about the two greatest commandments, the first of which tells us to love God with all your heart, mind, strength and soul."

"Bingo!" Wil jumped up from his seat. "You're right on target! But what does that mean, Jennifer?"

Apparently it was not a rhetorical question. He stood there smiling, waiting for an answer.

Suddenly Jennifer recalled a sermon Wil — Pastor Neilsen back then — had given right before he left First Baptist. She had kept the newsletter version in her Bible. It had ruffled a few feathers...

A MESSAGE FROM THE PASTOR

When you talk about loving someone - a parent or spouse or close friend - isn't it true that you go to lengths to try to serve them and honor them and do what's best for them. You learn their rules and expectations and values and you try to live up to them, right?

But do we do that with God? Not often! You know why? Because we haven't grasped what God was saying to us in Mark 12:30. We must love Him with all of our heart, mind, strength and soul. What does that mean?

When God says "heart," He is referring to your feelings and emotions. "Head" means intellect, ideas and thoughts. "Soul" is about your spirit - your moral convictions, your connection with Him. And "strength" deals with your actions, the things you do. When He tells us to love Him, He is not simply admonishing us to feel warm toward Him, or to empirically determine what He wants and give intellectual assent to it, or to go through the motions that convey some kind of tepid association with Him. He is exhorting you to allow Him to completely alter every dimension of your life.

If you do that, you are saying to yourself - and, of course, to Him - that you have such profound confidence and trust in Him that He can do as He wishes with you. In other words, you love Him! And the way He wants to transform you will not just bring Him joy but will radically redefine your life experience and bring you the highest levels of fulfillment and joy a human can possibly know.

Many of you are intellectuals. Your mind dominates your life. And I'll bet that because of that orientation, you have spent countless hours studying the Bible, memorizing passages of scripture, dissecting the major themes of the Word and tying them together. I bet you evangelize by trying to prove the truths of the gospel and by arguing people into Heaven. I bet you "love God" by acknowledging His greatness, publicly defending His nature and methods, and devoting yourself to learning more about Him. You're using your talents and gifts to honor God. You're maximizing your abilities within your comfort zone.

That's all good! But winning over your mind is not all He has planned for you. He wants you to have it all, but that means He wants to have all of you. And if you only give Him access to you from the neck up, He doesn't really have all of you, does He?

God wants you to work with you in the harder areas for you to manage, like your emotions and spirit and behavior.

In fact, He'd like to make it as easy as possible for you to flourish; He wants you to just give Him the whole job and let Him rip. Turn it all over to Him, lock, stock and barrel - or, in this case, heart, mind, strength and soul!

Give it up, everything, every aspect of who you are, not just the part that comes easiest to you!

In Christ,
PASTOR NEILSEN

OUTSIDE YOUR COMFORT ZONE

Jennifer realized Wil was still waiting for an answer.

"That ... our purpose is to love God and people?"

"Yeah, but that's just repeating the words..."

"Wait, Wil. You're not being fair," Jennifer retorted. She realized she sounded like one of his unhappy congregants who must have felt pinned down the way she was feeling right now. "I love God as best I can. I believe in Him, I understand His principles, I agree with them. I've committed myself to Him. Why isn't that enough?"

She felt tears building, and knew some of her anger was because of embarrassment.

"Jennifer, I'm sorry," Wil said, reaching out a hand to squeeze her shoulder. "I'm not calling you out! I'm just trying to explain that God wants it all. That's what the transformation process is!"

He smiled. "It's coming to the end of ourselves, realizing the horror of our defiance of God, diving deeper into ourselves than ever to seek His forgiveness, knowing that we cannot reform ourselves sufficiently for Him, realizing that only He can do that."

It began to dawn on Jennifer that maybe she was in a good spot, after all.

"Most people in your situation give up and lower the bar of their expectations. They settle for less than God's best. They climb back into their comfort zone and continue to move in circles for the rest of their life. They become churchy robots. And the body of Christ, as well as God, suffers for it."

The conversation had been intense, and Jennifer suddenly realized she felt wiped out. Dr. Neilsen had just challenged the very roots of her faith, and she had no idea where she was spiritually at this moment. But she understood that she was on the precipice of really understanding the meaning of salvation, God's love, and the selflessness that God has called us to embrace.

She shrugged and made a face that invited him to offer a direction.

Wil said moving down the transformation journey to a level most people never reach is not easy — in fact, it can get tougher, darker, and more confusing before reaching the great stuff.

"But this is the path that Jesus trod before us," he said. "Do you see that? He modeled all of this for us: the routines, the relationships, the challenges, the suffering, the doubt, the utter dependence upon God the Father before He reached that place of total peace, understanding, purpose and joy."

Wil looked intently at Jennifer. "I think that's where you're headed, if you're willing to declare war against yourself."

"What?" Jennifer was caught off guard.

"I mean, you need to decide to stop letting your habits and fears and self-centeredness misguide you. They're barriers to letting God transform you. Remember, you cannot transform yourself, and He will transform only if you cooperate with Him. He has a perfect plan for your life, but you must abandon your will — and pursue His will — for that plan to materialize."

Wil got up. "Does any of this make sense to you?"

She stood up and felt like she'd been run over by a Mack truck. All she could mumble was, "What do I do now?"

He gave her a gentle hug. "Well, remember, when Paul encourages us to work out our own salvation with fear and trembling, this is the process you go through. And don't take any of this from me alone. You said you were going to enlist some other sojourners in this process. That's terrific. Visit with them, get their counsel."

Jennifer gathered her things and turned toward the door.

"And above all, Jennifer, make God your partner in this part of the journey. Pray, but mostly by listening for His voice. Watch for the things He'll bring into your life. Read His word with a different lens — a filter that seeks to know what's next for you, if you're not in charge of the process. Remember, this is about love in the fullest — look at everything He gives you in terms of your relationship with Him and how He wants to transform you. Be alert. Take notes. Treat this as if it's the most important job you've ever done. I think you'll find that it is."

He paused and a huge smile filled his face. "You're His precious creation, Jennifer. It's gonna be great, you'll see. And thanks for letting me be part of the journey!"

NOVEMBER 18, 11 P.M.

Wow. My heart hasn't stopped racing, and my brain is still throbbing. I've got to write down things down. What were the most important points Dr. Neilsen made?

- I need to declare war against my nature to defeat my selfish nature and give God control.

- God wants to transform my life. I cannot do it without Him. He must lead the process and I must cooperate.

- My life has been too much about me. (That's for sure!) It needs to become focused on God.

- My salvation is not about getting what I want. It's about becoming who God made me to be — a needy person in love with and dependent upon Him.

- My ultimate goal may bring peace, joy and comfort, but the road there will be rocky and even painful.

I need to talk about this with someone. Who?

I know — Kevin and Kathy!

CHAPTER 5

RECOGNIZING OUR POWERLESSNESS

NOVEMBER 19, 10:15 A.M.

Just dialed up Kevin and Kathy! Great luck! They're home
tonight, and invited me to dinner! It was good to hear Kathy's
voice. She and Kevin may be quite a bit older than I am, but
they've been such good church friends that I don't even notice
the age difference.

I'm so glad they led my small group all those years. They are
probably the most spiritually together couple I know. And Kathy
makes a mean marinara sauce! Can't wait!

Jennifer, Kathy, and Kevin got caught up over a dinner of spaghetti
and meatballs. She was stunned to realize their kids were now
grown, living a few hours away, and with children of their own.
Only yesterday she had been their babysitter!

They moved to the front room with tea and Kathy's cookies. Kevin
got to the point and asked Jennifer about what she had been going

through. She so appreciated that, and how intently both he and Kathy listened to her answers.

Kevin leaned back in his La-Z-Boy.

"I've been rereading some of the Church's spiritual leaders. When you described your situation on the phone yesterday, I was reminded of Saint John of the Cross. Have you heard of him?"

Jennifer shook her head.

"Saint John of the Cross lived during the 1500s and was one of the great saints of the Church during the Middle Ages," he said in his learned but low-key manner. "He is best known for a book he wrote called *The Dark Night of the Soul*. Have you heard of it?"

Jennifer hadn't. She listened as Kevin described John's battle with what he called seasons of spiritual darkness.

"Sounds as if Dr. Neilsen and Saint John would agree on quite a bit. These were times when he was completely frustrated with his spiritual condition. His prayers seemed to float into the clouds, unanswered by God. His time with other believers seemed flat and worthless. When he worshiped God it didn't seem like there was any connection there. He served others but got no joy from it. He actually wondered where God was," Kevin said.

Now Jennifer was nodding.

"I guess you can relate, huh?" said Kevin, smiling. He leaned over to get his cup of coffee and took a sip before continuing. "But John also wrote about how important those tough times were because they taught him crucial lessons."

"What sort of lessons?" Jennifer asked.

"About our powerlessness, to start with," Kevin said. "We think we're giving it all to God, but the truth is, we are really counting on our abilities — our smarts, our muscle, our smooth talking, and all the rest — to get us where we think we need to go."

Kevin chuckled. "And Saint John wrote that we're not as smart or loving or godly as we like to think we are. John learned to thank God for those agonizing periods because it was the droughts that taught him how to depend on God more fully."

Kevin glanced at his wife. Kathy must have given him some sort of subtle signal, Jennifer decided, because Kevin shifted in his recliner and changed his tone.

"But here I am running off at the mouth, assuming things about your situation. Sorry, Jennifer. Things have been tough for you, huh?"

"Yes…" Jennifer was suddenly at a loss for words. "To be honest, I feel marooned in a spiritual black hole."

Kevin smiled. "Well, it probably doesn't help, but you aren't the first to feel that way, by a long shot. John also wrote about his spiritual poverty. He spoke about how he had to learn to renounce sin and selfishness, to accept deprivation as gift, and to redirect his mind and heart to prioritize a deeper union with God."

He leaned over the side of his chair, picked a worn book from a stack on the carpet next to his chair, and opened to one of several marked pages.

"Here's how one commentator summed up John's message. 'It's the shallow faith, the kind that focuses only on our happiness, that can't last. The times of darkness, the dark nights of the soul, ultimately serve to make our faith stronger and deeper.' " He chuckled. "Um-um. That's a heartache waiting to happen, isn't it?"

Something clicked in Jennifer's mind. "That reminds me of Bonhoeffer's cost of discipleship lessons that you taught us," Jennifer commented. She recalled that while studying the World War II German pastor's teachings she assumed they were about the connection between believers and the world. Now she saw that she would need to re-orient her thoughts more in terms of the relationship with God.

She made another connection. "And I vaguely remember something about John Wesley also having a life-changing moment once he recognized his spiritual poverty and humbled himself to serve God. Did I get that right?"

"Absolutely." Kevin beamed with pride.

Kathy stood up. "Time for some more tea," she said.

HAVING AN AFFAIR WITH GOD

Jennifer gathered her teacup and Kevin's, and followed Kathy to the kitchen.

Kathy took the teacups from Jennifer.

"Jennifer, do you remember our group discussion about death to self?" Kathy asked as she put the kettle on to boil. "I think it's a concept you may need to meditate on right now, to get through the wrestling match you're in."

Jennifer nodded. "I remember you and Kevin teaching that society says you have to rely on yourself to figure out everything and to get ahead, but that God says we are not little gods capable of winning the battle, that we have to partner with Him and let Him lead."

"Yes! We need to abandon our own grand personal ambitions in favor of His ambitions for His children, don't we?" Kathy said. She said that ultimately, it's not about having the most successful life by the world's terms, but about having the most surrendered life — on God's terms. Which means living very differently from what society expects.

"Our 'due north' in measuring how we're doing in life can't be material in nature. It has to be spiritual," Kathy said, plopping teabags in the teapot.

Kevin joined them. "That reminds me of 1 Peter 4:19. Remember, that's where the apostle Peter exhorts his friends to 'keep on doing what's right, and trust your lives to the God who created you, for He will never fail you'. But of course, doing that takes real truth and faith, which is where the rubber meets the road."

He leaned against the counter and described how often people back off when they realize they need to give God complete control of their lives. "That means that we resolve whatever situation we're facing — like the tension you're feeling in your life now — by choosing to live for God's agenda instead of our own."

"How countercultural," Jennifer interjected, smiling. "How un-American..."

"Yes! But the only alternative is to decide you'll handle this in your own way, on your own terms, and try to have a little bit of God on the side."

He laughed. "Good luck with that!"

Kathy laughed too. Jennifer looked at them both, slightly confused.

"Sorry, Jennifer," Kathy said, giving Jennifer a little hug. "That's a little in-house joke between me and Kevin. We talk about people who choose not to be transformed but still want to be Christian, kinda like having an affair with God. Rather than being fully devoted to Him, they do enough 'God stuff' to keep Him in the picture — but never at the center of the picture."

"Like a kind of secret, off-to-the-side relationship," Kevin said.

"Yeah. Kevin once told me it was the only affair he had to confess," she concluded, with a twinkle in her eye and a sly grin. "Want another cookie?"

NOVEMBER 19, 10:07 P.M.

Am I pretending to be having an affair with God? Ever since leaving Kevin and Kathy's, I've been thinking about that. Have I truly surrendered my life to Him? From what they were saying tonight, and from what Dr. Neilsen said, the answer is no.

That makes me feel a bit sick to my stomach — realizing how I'd messed up my relationship with God, but perhaps even more, realizing that moving ahead with Him is going to turn my life upside down!

Kathy said surrendering is the stumbling block for a lot of people. I can see that! We want it all — success, the experiences, fulfillment, reputation, comfort, and the rest.

And, like both Kevin and Kathy said, we're willing to sell our soul to get it.

What a thought!

We ask God to come along for the ride and we offer to let Him be part of what we're doing. Backwards!

And I've done that. I see that now. By keeping control of everything, and overestimating my capacity, I shut God out and have allowed Satan to pull my strings.

This is amazing to me. Like Kevin said, I've always thought I had to be strong and courageous, taking risks and going all out to master the world. But God made it very clear that we cannot control this world nor will we ever master it. Satan is the ruler of this domain and the only one who can overcome his cruel leadership is God Himself. We have to choose the right master in order to follow the right strategy and produce the right results.

Okay, I get this (sort of). But I'm still flummoxed (I love that word) because I truly believed that I <u>have</u> been committed to my faith in Jesus.

NOVEMBER 19, 11:27 P.M.

Can't get to sleep.

Why haven't I gotten over this speed bump and made it to the next stage of development? Kathy was nice to say she and Kevin were impressed with my dedication and passion to learn. But then she reminded me that we get so caught up in all the things we do, we forget that God is more interested in who we become than in what we achieve.

In fact, all the things we do for God usually wind up being

an obstacle to our relationship with Him! Isn't that a horrible thought!

Kevin said something else I want to remember. He said "we major on the minors." For example, we get all worked up about finishing a Bible study or remembering to pray or getting to the worship service on time. We're so obsessed with process and image and even with degrees of progress, that we forget why those actions matter in the first place — and for whom we're doing them.

In other words, all the religious things we do are routines we develop to make us look and feel like we're really spiritual and godly.

But the whole time we're knocking ourselves out finishing everything on our religious to-do list, God sits back and weeps because we're so intent upon doing "godly" things instead of becoming godly people.

That's why Kevin said this unattractive idea of surrender is so confusing but necessary. Americans think of surrender as weakness, when really it is wisdom revealing strength.

"If you do not surrender to God, Satan will keep you on his treadmill, pursuing worldly outcomes that never satisfy your mind, your heart or your soul," said Kevin. "It's one of the paradoxes of the Christian faith. When you're weak you're strong. When you surrender you eliminate confusion, anxiety, doubt, anger, frustration and distress. It has been remarkable."

That last statement caused me to sit up straight. Did they mean they had been through this transformation journey? These two, who seemed so experienced in Christ?

They both chuckled when I asked that. Kevin said, "We haven't been through the journey, Jennifer, we're still on the journey. Always will be."

He reminded me that life is a journey, not a destination. We reach the destination after the Lord relieves us of duty on earth. But then he answered my question more directly and said, yes, Kathy and he both went through what I'm going through now!

Wow! Then he said they learned about some of the possibilities when you decide to stick it out with God and truly let Him have His way with your life. I sensed that if I kept pushing for more I'd be opening up a real Pandora's Box. But what was my alternative? To continue to wallow in the muck of distress and dissatisfaction? I had to do this, even though emotionally it felt like I was entering a game with no rules.

So I mouthed the fateful words: "Tell me about that part of the journey."

CHAPTER 6

DISCOVERING WHAT IT TAKES

NOVEMBER 20, 10:15 A.M.

Kathy just called to ask if I was free tonight. They have a friend they want me to meet. She said there will be homemade cake to sweeten the deal. Yeah! I'll be there! (Even though I'm a little apprehensive. Okay, a lot.)

NO DISNEYLAND RIDE

The inviting aroma of fresh-baked chocolate cake helped soothe Jennifer's nerves when she arrived at Kevin and Kathy's that night. Kathy shooed her and Kevin to the breakfast nook in the kitchen, and set the gooey masterpiece in the middle of the table.

"Thanks for giving up another evening for me, you guys," Jennifer said as Kevin brought over four mugs and a carafe of hot decaf. Kathy plopped down plates, forks and napkins.

"Not at all, dear," Kathy replied. "But be ready to hear some things that you probably associate with fanatics, or the religious fringe. That's how transformed Christians come across to the rest of the world — and even to most church people," she said without any trace of rancor.

The doorbell rang. "That must be Lauren!"

In walked a woman around Jennifer's age, mid-thirties, African American, very fashionable. Through black designer eyeglasses she gazed at Jennifer and then smiled. "You must be Jennifer. Nice to meet you."

"You're just in time, Lauren," Kathy said. "I've been slapping Kevin's hands all evening, but now he gets to cut the cake!"

Kevin chuckled and grabbed the cake knife. "At last! Thank you, Lauren!"

With full plates and hot coffee, the four settled around the table and chatted for a while. Jennifer was impatient to bring up the evening's topic but didn't have to.

"Lauren, Jennifer has been asking about what it takes to be transformed by God," said Kevin. "You've had some experience with this, so I thought you could join in the conversation."

Lauren turned her gaze on Jennifer and smiled. "Put on your seatbelt, honey," she began, "because this ride is not sanctioned by Disneyland."

Everyone laughed, Jennifer a little nervously.

"No, really," Lauren said. "Allowing God to shape your life is the most amazing journey imaginable. Well, that's not really true, because until you're well down the track on this ride you can't really imagine what the journey is like! But, sure, I'd be happy to tell you what I've experienced."

She paused, took a deep breath and flashed a bittersweet smile.

"The key to advancing in this journey is brokenness. People have different ideas about what that means, but it's really just God shaking you up enough so that you see yourself realistically. It takes a lot more to shake up some people than others." She grinned. "From what Kevin and Kathy have said, you're probably one of those who need an earthquake."

Jennifer smiled and shrugged. She knew Lauren's hyperbole was from a kind heart.

Lauren continued. "With me, God grabbed my attention by confronting me with cancer."

A GUIDE THROUGH THE MINEFIELD

When Lauren was twenty-seven, she was diagnosed with pancreatic cancer. The disease appeared during a time in which Lauren already felt spiritually vulnerable. Things weren't going well in her life, and she didn't see God helping her as she thought He should. In fact, God didn't seem real anymore.

After the diagnosis came more testing, then the operations, the recovery, and months of grueling therapy and treatments. In the midst of this, Lauren's fiancé left her, and her father, who had been inactive in her life anyway, refused to visit. Then, at the end of her first stay in the hospital, she received an impersonal form letter telling her that her job had been reassigned and her services were no longer needed by the company she'd worked at for six years. The medical bills had already cleaned out her savings. And just when she thought there was no more bottom to drop out, two of her doctors came by late one night to give her their prognosis.

"It was absolutely shattering, and I bawled my head off. Here I was faced with the steady stream of large and incomprehensible bills for the medical care not covered by my health insurance — I'll be paying those off until the fourth of forever, by the way — and then, these two straight-faced, emotionless doctors sitting there coldly handing me a list of permanent physical limitations I'd have to live with. I was completely overwhelmed.

"And it was the best thing that could ever happen to me."

"What?" Jennifer put down her fork. She looked hard at Lauren, then Kathy and Kevin.

"God used it to break you, didn't He?" Kevin said quietly.

"Yes!" Lauren sat straight up in her chair, raised her fists in a touch-down sign. "That's exactly why my bout with cancer was so wonderful. God got my attention! He shook me up, and then we got busy! I wouldn't wish the pain and limitations on anybody, but I wouldn't trade it for anything."

"What do you mean, 'we got busy'?" Jennifer asked.

"Listen, I was a mess. I was totally upset with God and made no effort to hide my feelings. I felt it wasn't fair: I was too young, too good a person, had too much unfulfilled potential, just wasn't strong enough to handle all of this. When I thought about what the doctors said, or looked in the mirror at what I'd become, I was angry that I wasn't the Lauren I used to be, and never would be again. I fluctuated between two emotions: angry and hurting."

She took a sip of coffee. "But because of being helpless and flat on my back and alone, I had to examine a lot of things in my life. My bottom-line conclusion was that I was not big enough to defeat the disease — and God was my only hope. That led me to realize that up to that point, I had been using God for my own purposes."

"Using God? How?" Jennifer asked. "You don't seem to be a manipulator."

"Oh, I knew *about* Him but I really didn't know Him. I *said* I loved Him but I really didn't. Even when I prayed I was usually telling Him my plans and expecting Him to bless them, or passing on my requests and citing scriptures to box Him into giving me what I wanted. I had no interest in what He had designed for my life and had no clue how to pick His voice out of the crowd. I probably wouldn't have followed it anyway, unless it told me what I wanted to hear. It's no wonder I felt spiritually stuck and frustrated. I was trying to call the shots in a world I didn't control."

Jennifer dropped her head. Lauren had just described her perfectly. She started to feel nauseous. She squeaked out another question. "What did you do next?"

"Oh, this is the good part, Jennifer. The first thing I had to do was apologize for my selfishness and for relegating Him to, I don't know, probably about tenth place on my priority list. Then, of course, I had to figure out how to make room for Him in my life. My existence was so crowded there was just no free space in which to put Him. Remember, I was all about using Him when I needed Him. There was no ongoing relationship. It was all about me. He was a value-added acquaintance.

"And then it struck me. There I was again, trying to fit God into *my* framework, making Him conform to *my* world. What I really needed was a complete makeover: new thought patterns, new priorities, new habits, new purpose, new relationships, new values, everything new. And that's just what happened. It was like being reborn."

That phrase lit Jennifer up. "Wow. Let me ask about that, Lauren. A friend of mine talked to me about the fact that a lot of us misunderstand the whole 'born again' thing, what God's offer of salvation by grace is really about. Did you go through any doubts about your salvation?"

"Are you kidding me?" Lauren shook her head as she laughed. "Sure did! While I was in that hospital bed with all those machines and tubes connected to me I thought a lot about salvation. And it occurred to me that the reason He saved me wasn't just to keep me out of Hell. His purpose was for me to love Him and to enjoy being with Him on earth as well as in Heaven."

Lauren went on to describe how she reflected on all the lessons and Bible passages she had learned over the years. It dawned on her that what she was going through was part of the war between God and Satan. Satan wanted to keep her in bondage. He was accomplishing that by distracting her from God and by elevating the pleasure and importance of other things in her life. While she was bedridden with her disease, she didn't have all the stuff that keeps us so busy — the technology, the media, the meetings, the opportunities, the perks. That gave her space to clear her head and rethink her purpose.

"My illness forced me into a simple lifestyle. That helped me to see life more clearly. So between being scared about my life, scared about my soul, scared about everything, I decided that I had really missed the point of life all along! That's when I chose to redirect my path."

"Okay, but exactly what does that mean?" Jennifer was starting to feel impatient. She desperately wanted specifics. "What did that redirection look like?"

"Well for starters, it meant I had to really give Him my *life*. When I accepted Christ as my savior I *said* I was making Him the Lord of my life — heck, I even *thought* I was doing that, because of all my church routines and spiritual activity — but I really didn't. He wasn't number one — not by a long shot. So I promised myself I'd eliminate all the distractions that kept my eyes off Him, my ears incapable of Hearing Him, my heart from loving Him, my lifestyle from honoring Him."

She could see Jennifer's frustration level rising, so she took it down a notch.

"Okay, specifically: Less media — TV, movies, music, video games. They don't really add value to my life, they anesthetize me. More prayer — and less of it featuring me talking, more of it spent listening for His voice or seeking His guidance, through the subtle ways He communicates. Different friends — people who are on the same quest, who have the same yearning to know God intimately. Being less ambitious professionally — doing my tasks with excellence but not putting so much energy and hope into being the rising star of the work crowd."

Lauren took a sip of coffee and captured the last cake crumbs on her plate. This was the kind of hands-on detail Jennifer hungered for. She had had enough of the theory and theology.

Finally, here is a survivor sharing the location of the landmines.

"Next I had to find a *serious* church — one that values this kind of spiritual commitment and would provide sincere encouragement and practical help in becoming more like Jesus. And as little as I wanted it, I recognized that I needed some real accountability from trustworthy, spiritually mature people. This process has introduced me to some wonderful people I've let into my life, being open to them examining my life at any time and in any way they choose. I need them to keep me on track with not just my behavior but also my pursuit of God."

When Lauren paused again for another gulp of java, Jennifer asked, "What else?" She was almost afraid to hear the answer. *Isn't there any stone in this process that goes unturned?*

Lauren described how she had to develop a brand new attitude toward God, in which she regularly rediscovered humility and wept with gratitude over His love. Now her commitment to regular times of silence and solitude in the presence of the Lord had become a top priority.

"I can honestly say now that I think of my time with Him as the best hours of the day, not a burdensome fulfillment of my obligation. Another big change is that I've learned to interact with the Bible differently as well," she said.

No longer did she treat the Bible as a religious reference book, but as His love letter to her. Her reason and logic used to get in the way of deepening her relationship with God through the Word. Now the Bible provided encouragement as well as unexpected revelation as the Holy Spirit gave her instruction.

"I could go on, Jennifer," Lauren said. "But the question is, do you really want me to?"

AFTER THE BROKENNESS

Jennifer sat in stunned silence. Lauren hadn't just undergone a makeover; she was a new person.

That explained why she was so different from other Christians. Less hurried, more reflective, not as devoted to getting ahead in the work world despite her obvious intelligence and stellar education, and less wired into the bustle of church activity without being any less intense about her devotion to God.

Jennifer sensed this was the real stuff she'd been searching for — not easy or comfortable or perhaps even do-able, but real and authentic. She sat mulling things over.

People always told Jennifer that she was easy to read. Maybe that's why Kevin chimed in after a couple minutes of silence.

"Jennifer, like Lauren, both Kathy and I turned the corner on cooperating with God once we realized that transformation is mostly God's doing. What we contribute is an unqualified acceptance of His love, a total openness to letting Him have His way with us, trusting Him to do what's best for us. We also found that it was important to renew that commitment every single day, more for our benefit than His, of course. He does the rest, if you let Him. Does this make sense?"

Jennifer lifted her head and looked at Lauren. "It's beginning to, but to be honest, God putting people through such trials to be broken seems almost cruel, especially if His objective is to draw us closer to Him."

Lauren just smiled, looking tranquil.

Kevin jumped in. "Well, it may seem that way to us, but it's certainly not uncommon. I've read research that shows that God uses tragedies and crises to position people for such an awakening."

He recounted that something like half of the people who get serious about cooperating with God in the transformation process were motivated, like Lauren, to do so by experiencing a major tragedy: a life-threatening or debilitating illness or injury, a hotly-contested divorce, the prolonged and painful death of a very close loved one, a bankruptcy or business failure, imprisonment, or the loss of one's material possessions in a disaster.

"The other half who move forward on the journey were fortunate or wise enough to enter the stage of brokenness without a precipitating tragedy."[12]

A thought struck Jennifer. "Do you think my spiritual discomfort and frustration means I'm about to experience one of those kinds of crises?"

She realized nobody could foretell the future, but she was mesmerized by the fact that half of those on the journey were awakened by such a tragedy.

Kevin's eyes crinkled. "I'd wager that the restlessness you're feeling these days is because you're distracted from God and not giving Him free rein to move you toward holiness."

He leaned over and rested his hand on top of hers. "You clearly have good intentions, but the busyness and ambitions of your life are getting in the way of God's best for you. He wants all of your mind, your heart, your strength and your soul, Jennifer, not just what's left over after work, or before Pilates."

Kathy was nodding. "Jennifer, we've known you a long time, so I'll be frank. I think you've reached the point where you now have to determine what's most important to you: your commitment to God or your commitment to yourself."

NOVEMBER 20, 10:37 P.M.

I am wiped out. Tonight was great, but I'm so tired. So much to think about. After Kathy's blunt ultimatum, I just wanted to go home!

Kevin said not to be discouraged, because God desperately wants me to move forward and won't prevent me from making progress on the journey. That's not to say that He won't put me through some hoops. But like Kevin said, if I get stuck and can't figure out why, I'm supposed to look in the mirror. "The culprit will be there, staring back at you," Kevin said.

Wow. No pressure...

I was reminded tonight of Tozer writing that there's an inverse relationship between how comfortable we are with the world and how close we are to Jesus. [13] We're supposed to know ourselves well enough to examine and diagnose our condition and then prescribe the remedy. That, Kevin said, is my next step.

Oh, is that all?

Before I left their house, I asked if there are there other people they know who have also been through this. People they could recommend who are also on this journey.

They of course corrected me, saying everyone is on the journey. Unfortunately, most people never get as far as accepting Christ as their savior. Among those who do, some enter God's kingdom broken by their sin, so their process moves a little quicker past this phase that I'm in. But most claim Christ as their savior without really being brokenhearted about their sins. The restless stage I'm in now becomes the barrier they never overcome. Some are stymied by ignorance. Some settle for a mediocre spiritual life — even after getting good counsel or discovering through God's Word or other means of revelation that they have to get radically right with God. That requirement in itself halts their progress. How sad.

Still, Kevin mentioned a few people who have gone through the dark period and come out of it ready to move forward with the Lord. Like Brian, the pastor to seniors at church, and Michael, Kevin and Kathy's accountant. Thank goodness Lauren piped up.

She mentioned Lucas, that tall dark-haired guy who plays guitar in the worship band at church. She said he has had a pretty amazing journey. And she also named Evan, the guy that works down at The Coffee Shack, the tall guy with the long black hair, who's always smiling at customers.

I think I'll go visit The Coffee Shack.

NOVEMBER 20, 11:54 P.M.

One last thing. Both Kevin and Kathy reminded me that this isn't a task that someone can complete overnight. When God transforms someone's life, it takes time, kind of like aging a good wine or fine wheel of cheese. It cannot be rushed, as much as we'd like to hurry it along sometimes.

In fact, Kathy described watching some people get to the point of breaking through to the maturity end of the continuum, only to see them regress because they were too impatient.

I wonder if I'll get too impatient. Or rebellious.

Transformation, they said, is rarely a forward-only process. Kevin said to expect to get stuck in some ruts along the way. But he said it's like having engine trouble in your car while you're on a long distance trip. You're stopped but you don't have to abandon the car. You have to do some unexpected things and rearrange your plans before you can resume the journey, but if you're willing to do those things, at the appropriate time you can move ahead.

Of course, once the car is fixed, you can either turn around and return to where you came from or you can continue forward toward your desired destination. There's no requirement that you keep moving forward, and if you do, there is always a price to pay for new ground gained.

I think I secretly had been hoping I'd hear tonight that my restlessness was merely a sign I needed a vacation!

Or at least some fresh new teachings or something.

What I have gotten from Dr. Neilsen, Kevin and Kathy, and Lauren is way more than I bargained for. Now what?

CHAPTER 7

MY HEART FINALLY BROKE

NOVEMBER 24, 7:54 A.M.

At last, the Thanksgiving break is here. I need the time off to get myself together. I haven't slept well since my evening with Kevin, Kathy and Lauren — and I really hadn't had a good night's sleep since talking to Wil. (I still have trouble calling Dr. Neilsen by his first name!)

I'm exhausted. I'm distracted. I have to get a grip on this transformation thing. I plan to do three things over the four-day break: sleep, pray, and think.

NOVEMBER 24, 8:17 P.M.

I need to record this IM exchange with Wil. If I'm honest with myself, it was my last-ditch effort to avoid having to be broken by God, although I still don't know what that will look like. Wil was helpful, even if he didn't provide the response I was hoping for. (What WAS I hoping for?)

> *JENNIFER:* Wil, I was saved almost 10 years ago. Wasn't that evidence of my parting with sin, and of my brokenness before God?

WIL: Did you go through a time of mourning or some kind of self-confrontation experience over how you had treated God up to that point?

JENNIFER: I was thrilled to know that God forgave me of all my sins, even if I didn't really understand the full scope of what was being given to me. After that point I really tried to be a different, better, more godly person.

WIL: That's great, but it doesn't address what I asked. How did you respond — emotionally, intellectually, physically, and spiritually — upon being forgiven and receiving the Holy Spirit?

(At that point I realized that if I couldn't bluff a mentor into believing I'd been through my heartbreak stage, I sure wasn't going to fool God into buying my act. After admitting as much to Wil, he continued with a related line of inquiry.)

WIL: Let me ask you this. Have you ever imagined your life without God?

JENNIFER: This is a theological trick question, right? Life without God is impossible. God has always existed and has always been part of my life, whether I knew it or not.

WIL: That wasn't meant to trip you up. Theologically your statements are true. But I'm asking about your mind and heart. At any time since you admitted your sins and asked Jesus to save you, have you imagined what your life would be like if He were not part of it?

JENNIFER: No, I guess not. Why?

WIL: It's an exercise that's been helpful to people I know who have been transformed. Difficult one, though. We generally ignore Him until we're in trouble or want something really badly. Until He grabs our attention through some pretty dramatic means we are usually happy to go on at arm's length, pretending we're close to Him, but treating Him more like a professional colleague than our omnipotent Father. If you imagine what your life would be like without His love, protection, guidance, promises, hope, and all the rest He provides, it's a pretty mind-boggling reorientation of our lives.

JENNIFER: OK, I'll think about that one...

WIL: BTW, I'm not trying to judge you or play holier than thou. Just passing on some tips I've picked up along the way...

JENNIFER: No worries, I appreciate it. I need all the help I can get.

WIL: Remember, the Bible calls us to do what we have to in order to conform to Christ's image. The good news is, we *can* do it — with His help. The bad news, sort of, is that it's a monster of a task. It usually requires a radical purging of desires, expectations, habits, values and beliefs. This is part of the never-ending part of the journey.

JENNIFER: Thanks, Dr. Neilsen. I appreciate your time and wisdom.

WIL: Got another minute?

JENNIFER: Sure, no hurry here.

WIL: Have you thought about your purpose in life? One of the foundational perspectives missing as people seek Him is an understanding of their God-given life's purpose. We often confuse gifts and abilities with purpose. We all have the same purpose in life: to love God and love His people with all of our mind, heart, spirit and effort. It's HOW we do that that makes each of us unique. We each possess different experiences, information, relationships, gifts and talents toward that end. But grasping our true purpose, right from the start, helps us get on track about our relationship with Him. Our purpose is to live for Him, not to do everything we can to squeeze the most out of life. He makes the most of our life if we turn it over to Him.

JENNIFER: That was worth an extra minute. Thanks.

WIL: OK. Night Jennifer. Be strong and courageous...

REASONING IT OUT

Jennifer sank into her favorite overstuffed chair. The pumpkin pie she had made for the family gathering this afternoon was in the oven. She pulled out her journal and reread recent entries. She knew that it was time to use her widely lauded "Jennifer Logic" to crack the code.

Finishing my master's thesis was easier than articulating what this transformation is, she thought. *Fortunately there is no academic committee I have to defend my conclusions to. On second thought, maybe that's what the Trinity is...*

She started to write.

- Transformation is not optional, it's required, if I want to make the most of my life.

- I am incapable of transforming my life; I must choose to cooperate and partner with God in that process.

- What about salvation? I may or may not be saved; it's kind of unclear to me at this point. I said the sinner's prayer, was baptized and got involved in a church, but was my heart broken by my offenses toward God? Not really. Did I transition from knowing about God to longing for intimacy with Him? Not really. Do I have a deep, constant, two-way connection with Him? Not really. It seems pretty clear that I need to invest myself more fully in my relationship with God — He wants it, I need it; I hope to get to the place where I want it as badly as He does.

- God wants to draw us to Him. He is so determined to give us every chance to become who He wants us to become that He'll go to huge lengths to draw us closer to Him. Part of the time He'll wait until our hearts break, not because of a dramatic experience but because we recognize the implications of our sin and reach a point of intensely desiring to know Him. From that point we finally commit to going deep with Him. Part of the time, though, we're too defiant to see how things really are, too stubborn to go all out in repentance and connection. Then He'll allow drastic circumstances in our lives as a wake-up call to shake us into dependence upon Him. I sure don't want to go there! And I certainly don't want to be part of the majority who experience those circumstances and still decide to go it alone, without Him as a partner.

Jennifer put down her pen for a moment and rolled her shoulders. *I'm too smart, too scared, and too wimpy to do that! she thought. Looks like I'll have to pursue Him the old-fashioned way — through reason rather than experience. I guess that'd be going the way of Paul (he of the "come, let us reason" approach) instead of David (the guy caught in adultery, guilty of murder, baby son dies).*

She smiled at her own cleverness and glanced at her watch. Twenty-five more minutes until she had to take the pie out of the oven. She went back to her notebook.

- <u>To grow, I have to fully love God and love people</u> — really love them — on <u>four levels</u>: my thoughts about them, my feelings toward them, my actions affecting them, and how my spirit responds to them. I do not fully love them until I have focused my four capacities on the purity and depth of my relationship with them.

- <u>Loving God:</u> Among other things this means that my love for God cannot simply be the kind of intellectual love I've had, or the emotional love others have, but must be a viable blend of loving Him through what I know about Him, how I feel about Him, what I do for Him and with Him, and how I surrender my spirit and will to Him. This kind of multi-faceted, balanced love is foreign to me — and to most people — but my love for Him won't be real until I bring these four dimensions of myself into a more perfect union.

- The journey to optimal transformation: Those traveling on this journey can look forward to peace, joy and comfort. But the road there will be characterized by difficult moments: pain, suffering, confusion, anxiety, fear, loneliness, sorrow, despair, frustration and disappointment. If I sincerely want a breakthrough, I will have to tough it out; there is no alternative to sharing in the suffering and harshness that Jesus experienced when He absorbed my sins and agreed to be my sacrifice to God.

- My life has been too much about me; it needs to become focused on God.

- Transformation is not a linear, straightforward journey. It is normal to gain ground, lose some of it, win it back and then some, lose a bit of that, and so forth — the old three-steps-forward, two-steps-back routine. Diligence is an indispensable quality for this journey — but you can only gin up that kind of perseverance if it's motivated by a longing for, and absolute trust in, God.

- What I've learned at church: I'm still not sure if the teachings and experiences I've had through church will prove to be helpful, or harmful. Based on what I've heard, maybe some of each.

- Church: My church might even be an impediment to maturity — I have to really think about this one — but I have to be open to being part of a community of faith that is not just playing religious games and giving lip service to God, but is sold out to transformation. I'm getting the sense that's more unusual than I would have imagined.

- What I may have to relearn: Like, how to read the Bible. The objective is not for me to master information, but for the Holy Spirit to master me through my absorption of its truths and directives. Like how to pray: spending more time listening and pondering than telling God what I think or want. Like worshiping: making it a continual conversation with God, recognizing His presence and greatness all around me, instead of showing up on Sundays to sing and take notes (although I think that still counts).

- <u>My thoughts and feelings</u> will have to adjust quite a bit. I knew intellectually that Jesus turned people's thinking upside down, but I don't think I've ever allowed Him to turn my thinking and emotions upside down. Unless I let Him do so, this train ain't leavin' the station.

The kitchen timer buzzed. Jennifer inhaled the sweet, earthy aroma of pumpkin pie. Jumping up, she plopped her notebook on the seat of the chair with a flourish of resolve.

So my next challenge is to figure out where I stand — and where I want to stand. Am I really ready to redefine my understanding of the Christian life? Of me? That's where I think all of this is leading...

JANUARY 1, 9:34 A.M.

Well, Thanksgiving and Christmas have come and gone, and I'm setting aside New Year's Day to catch up on what's happened.

This week was a turning point for me. I have definitely decided that I need to move forward on this journey!

(Really, what's the alternative? I can be like most people and wimp out or I can trust God when He says He has a beautiful (if occasionally gnarly) future for me if I just let Him take control of the steering wheel of my life. So I'm handing it over to Him. I've never been much of a driver, anyway.)

The big challenge looming before me now is to evaluate and make right my relationship with God.

I think this is my next hurdle: to have a longing to know Him, to choose to spend most of my time with Him, to become insep-arable from Him. Like Kathy said. Kinda like I always imagined marriage would be like.

JANUARY 1, 12:12 P.M.

These last few weeks, as I have pondered my past, I realized that I have never allowed myself to be that vulnerable with Him or to become dependent upon Him. But that is what's in store for me. The good news is, I know He wants this connection with me too, so it will happen. I can have faith in that!

I've also spent some time combing through the Bible, seeking insight into "brokenness." On its own, the term seems unappealing, sterile and procedural. I need to discover the emotional and spiritual sides of the process. I have been reading and rereading, meditating and praying through these verses — begging God for keener insight into them and a divine wisdom about how to apply them.

Here's what strikes me so far from living with these passages for a while.

It's all about serious love.

I think Dr. Neilsen hit the nail on the head when he talked about loving God and people as fully as possible through an integrated combination of thinking, feeling, doing and spirit. Mark 12:30-31 makes that clear.

Just as clear is the fact that I'm not there yet. If Jesus said these are the most important commands, then they are, period. I think everything else flows from here. I want to get in the flow.

Only God can restore me, and only after I've genuinely repented.

While reading the psalms by David (a broken man) and the warnings of the prophets (Jeremiah, Isaiah and Joel), it became clear that admission of my sins and submission to the appropriate punishment must precede God's compassionate restoration.

My heart must break with agony and cry out for forgiveness

before He can show His mercy. Joel 2:12-13 as well as Psalms 38:3-7 and 51:2-4 sum up where I need to be.

Wallow in sorrow.

I've never been one to linger on any emotion — well, any helpful ones — but after reading a series of scriptures, I have a new appreciation for how important deep, true sorrow is to God. Jeremiah is the clearest vessel of this expectation of God. The weeping prophet describes the necessary response to sin as mourning, crying, grieving, despair, pain and remorse.

I've got to feel this in my gut; it ought to make me double over in suffering and put me on the verge of depression. It's not emotion for its own sake; this needs to be emotion born out of the pain of knowing that I have severely wounded the one who gave up His life for me.

In retrospect, I have felt bad because I knew what I did was wrong. I felt guilty. I felt embarrassed because I've been caught. But I don't think I've taken this relationship so seriously that I have been intellectually, emotionally, spiritually and physically devastated for cheating on my eternal lover, for defying and rejecting the only one who has ever or will ever love me without conditions or even a demand for reciprocity.

It reminds me of a Disney fairy tale: my prince has come and I was too busy primping in front of the mirror to notice or to bother answering when he knocked. This is beginning to help me get a grip on the "woe to you" passages in Matthew 23.

I can fool me but I can't fool Him.

Since I said the prayer to accept Jesus as my savior, I've believed that I was so thankful that I had really repented and was undeniably in love with God. The more I ponder the depth of His demonstrated love for me, and how He pictures true love in the Bible, the more I realize my self-deception.

For almost a decade I have been an actor in an evolving religious play, and I deserve an Oscar for my portrayal of a repentant sinner reformed by the grace of God and immersed in His work for His glory. I suspect I have received a standing ovation from everyone but God. He knows my heart. He is not fooled and cannot be mocked by my amateurish attempt to persuade Him of my sincerity. Jeremiah 17:9-10 reveals that He knows my real love and secret motives. I am so busted!

I need to die to myself.

How often this theme is repeated in the scriptures! But until I developed the eyes to see it, this concept was invisible to me.

John described the need as me getting smaller so God could get bigger in my life (John 3:30). Paul wrote the epistle to the Romans about this very matter, poignantly describing the need in Romans 2:8. Paul further wrote about this in other epistles, such as 2 Corinthians 5:17, which asserts that we are becoming a new person in Christ — which, of course, cannot happen until we dispose of the old one!

No more talk, just proof.

I suppose God gets a steady blast of prayers from people who are trying to convince Him they've changed. His response is unequivocal: show me you've changed by how differently you now live. (Matthew 3:8)

The best proof is how diligently I fight against sinful responses. I have dismissed the fact that this is a real war to win me over. (Ephesians 6:10-11) It sounds ridiculous, but both God and Satan are wooing me: God with genuine love and care,

Satan with attractive but destructive enticements and carefully packaged empty promises.

Am I sufficiently humble before the God of all creation? No. Have I devoted myself to fierce resistance of anything that smacks of sin, evil or the devil's entrapments? No. (James 4:7-8) Have I been a loyal bride of the ultimate groom? No. Have I dedicated myself to eradicating every trace of impurity in my life, as a gift to my divine father, protector, lover and counselor? No. Have I exhausted myself slaying the evil desires and passions planted in my life by the deceiver? No. (Galatians 5:24-25)

Well, Jennifer, honey, it's time to put up or shut up. This charade has gone on long enough. It's time to play the final round of Who Do You Really Love? and declare a winner.

It's really not about me.

Paul got it when he wrote in Romans 14:7-8: "We don't live for ourselves or die for ourselves. If we live, it's to honor the Lord. And if we die, it's to honor the Lord. So whether we live or die, we belong to the Lord."

That pretty much sums it up, doesn't it? It's a good time for me to get over me and get onto Jesus.

A CLEARER VIEW

By the end of the first week of the new year, Jennifer desperately wanted to share a new train of thought with someone she knew would get it. So she decided to surprise Kevin and Kathy with an old-fashioned letter.

January 7
Dear Kevin and Kathy:

I've spent hours over the past couple of weeks doing something I've never done before: reviewing my sins! Really! Not just those I committed in the past day or two; all of the sins I can remember committing throughout my life. Sins when I was a kid. Sins when I was in high school. The indiscretions of my college years. The secret things of my post-college experience. Fun, huh?

And my recitation has incorporated my offenses against God in relation to family, friends, anonymous people, organizations, church, my employers and clients, teammates and opponents, teachers, doctors, and so on.

The list encompasses things I've said, thought and done. Of course, having ignored most of my sins at the time of, or directly after, their commission, I have had a lot of trouble figuring out a way to recall them. I finally hit on an approach that worked for me: going through the Ten Commandments, one by one, identifying as many times that I broke each of the ten as possible.

That isn't as quick as I thought it'd be, because I actually had to study up on what each of them meant!

For instance, the first, second and third commandments. I had to spend a bunch of time figuring out that not having any god other God or worshiping any idols or imagery addresses some of my infatuations, obsessions and "guilty pleasures" that are considered normal in our society. I've had a humbling time of identifying and repenting for a wide range of values and pursuits, from my must-see TV shows, non-negotiable snack foods, and celebrity worship to my body image fixations, anxieties about finances and retirement funds, and even my secret worship of my reasoning abilities.

If you ever want to get depressed, recite your sins, from the beginning of your life to the present. You'll be astounded at what a low-life scoundrel you are. I don't recommend it as a parlor game or a conversation starter for a first date.

But wait, there's more! Here's yet another option on the self-flagellation parade. I even asked family members and friends to be honest with me and list some of the things I've done that have hurt them or that they've observed me do that have hurt others.

Yikes, what an eye opener that was! A few people refused to

play along, saying they've never observed anything inappropriate. (I'm writing that down so that if they ever ask me to help them identify their sins I can make sure *that* lie is on the list!) But once people understood what I was attempting to do, and realized that it wasn't a trick or some sneaky way of getting them to reveal their own shortcomings, they got into it. Maybe they felt like they were ministering to me. I guess in a weird way they were. After all, I'd asked for it and it related to my spiritual growth.

Why beat myself up this way? I felt convicted by Romans 8:32, where Paul gives the famous and widely misused verse about the truth setting us free. Jesus is the Truth, and He will indeed set us free -- if we will confront the sins that necessitated the Son of God coming to earth and dying in my place because of those very sins.

So for me, at least, it is important to recognize the breadth and depth of who I have been so I can have a clearer view of who I want to become. Some people obsess over their family tree: they have a deep-rooted need to know where they came from. In a way, this sin review is a variation on that theme: this is where I've been, where I've come from. Including a lot of places I don't want to admit and I don't want publicly known. Even by you guys!

You see, if someone tells a lie here or slams someone there, or occasionally disobeys parents -- well, none of that seems like such a big deal. (Of course, it is to a holy and righteous God whose original desire was to inform us of the rules so we wouldn't sin at all, before He restructured things due to the extent of our limitations.) But when you add it all up, it's a real hammer blow to the head! It's not a pretty picture, and I hate to see all of this put together, but it has certainly helped me better understand the significance of Jesus's death and resurrection and what a magnificent act of grace His enduring love for us represents.

Love, Jennifer

JANUARY 14, 4:07 P.M.

Have you ever stopped to dig deep into the effects of sin in your life?

If you gave me a Sunday school exam, I probably would have scored well on the effects — and thought nothing more about the personal implications. But as I've been cruising down Sin & Sorrow Street recently, I've had to get more than a superficial understanding.

After all, if my heart is supposed to be broken and my life turned upside down by the damage my sins have done, it's crucial to know what difference the commission of sin makes in my life.

So, I collected the following list. Sin:

- Separates me from a holy and loving God.
- Dulls my decision-making acuity.
- Bogs me down with guilt and reduces my self esteem.
- Diminishes my quality of life.
- Undermines my judgment.
- Substitutes comfort for conscience.
- Minimizes people's (or God's) trust in me.
- Automatically raises questions about my motives.
- Improves my capacity to manipulate and exploit people.
- Increases my stress levels because I try to appear clean and pure.

If you were to ask me if those are the outcomes I want characterizing my life, I'd say no in a heartbeat. But if I continue down Sin & Sorrow Street that's where I'm headed. It is becoming more clear to me that I need to turn a major corner, and take the transformational journey to its end point.

CHAPTER 8

STARTING TO GET IT

JANUARY 25, 7:09 A.M.

The new year has not been shaping up as a happy period in Jennifer's Journey.

For weeks — after returning from work or on weekends — I've been ruminating on who I am, what I've done to God, who I need to change into. The poor people who live below me are probably tired of my pacing.

On the one hand there's the socially desirable expectation — of course I'll choose to love God with all my heart, mind, strength, and soul, and then to love others that same way.

On the other hand we have reality: that I just might not have the courage or diligence to do it. This whole confrontation has me wound up like a corkscrew.

FEBRUARY 5, 11:04 A.M.

What a huge shift this wholehearted turn to Jesus represents. I know some of my reticence is because I'm being wooed by a world-class deceiver, Satan. He's had me pretty much to himself up to this point and is not about to give me up without a fight.

Strangely, I know all of this intellectually, but I haven't coordinated my head with my heart yet. If you look at it objectively, it's so black and white: do I choose God, the compassionate and forgiving lover of my soul, or Satan, the malicious deceiver who wants to keep me in bondage until a time of desolation and destruction? Objectively speaking, it's not much of a contest. But humans are rarely objective about anything; I certainly am not.

My reflections on transformation have also uncovered a consistent strategic error on my part. Rather than obsess on Satan — his schemes, his goals, his tactics, his effectiveness — I ought to maintain a strong focus on God and what He wants for and from me. In the midst of the distractions and deceptions of the world, that's so hard! It turns out I'm a lot more easily seduced by tangents and peripherals than I'd ever imagined.

FEBRUARY 15, 9:22 P.M.

There actually is quite a bit of writing on the transformation journey. I've been paying particular attention to what authors have said about the process of being broken by our sin and our detachment from God.

One of the ideas that resonated within me was to not only recognize that we are made to be relational — belonging is one of the most basic human needs — but that studies have shown the people who thrive are those who have significant, healthy connections. I may have a bunch of good friends, but if I'm not connected to the ultimate source of true life and meaning, health and sustenance, then where am I really headed?

And to be theologically correct, if it's all about God and not me, then I have to turn that around and begin by wondering what He truly desires from me and how I can satisfy that need, because that's the only avenue through which I'll achieve any lasting and genuinely satisfying fulfillment and joy.

FEBRUARY 23, 5:06 P.M.

I've been reading some of Saint Augustine's stuff, too. It's rather heavy, and I can't take too much at each sitting. But it's pretty rich material.

One of the lasting challenges he gave me was to identify the things that give me joy in life and notice who provided those to me.

I identified the enjoyment I get from being at the ocean or in the mountains; the beauty and serenity of a clear blue sky with puffy white clouds; happiness I feel when I see a garden brimming with orange-red marigolds. I thought about how much I love to eat bananas and nectarines, or drink a delicate white zinfandel. Some of my favorite memories are of watching a wall of pink and gray clouds shape-shift above the sun as it disappears into the ocean on a distant horizon.

The list went on and on, but I discovered that these were His love gifts to me — things He created for my pleasure and to help me understand Him as He expressed Himself through them. [14]

For more than three decades I have enjoyed these special gifts but I have taken them for granted and snubbed the giver. If I had children who behaved that way I'd spank them, ask what they were thinking, and give them a major timeout! But it turns out that I am that ungrateful brat. (I'm giving myself a suspended sentence...)I don't know about experiencing sorrow, but I'm sure getting slammed with a deadly dose of guilt.

MARCH 15, 10:02 P.M.

I just finished reading a book about spiritual growth and disciplines. One critical statement really got to me: feel sorry but not guilty.

Guilt produces continued sin. It just encourages us to keep doing what we've been doing because we feel worthless, rebellious, misunderstood, abandoned, whatever. The point of being a child of God, a child of the King no less, is that He forgives us and elevates us beyond that guilt.

So it's okay for me to recognize my sin, but I cannot let Satan impale me on guilt; better to feel sorry for what I've done, so sorry that I authentically repent — turn away from those actions — and commit to doing things differently in the future because of my love for the one I have sinned against.

As of this moment I'm done with guilt. On to sorrow...

BROTHER LOVE

"Hey, Jenny, what's goin' on? The Drewmeister here."

It was Jennifer's younger brother, Andrew. The guy who never found a party he wouldn't crash or never met a girl he wouldn't, well, you know.

"Haven't heard from ya for a while. You OK?" he asked in his goofy, upbeat, faux-surfer boy patter.

"Yup, doin' just great, Andrew." *Keep the answers short and sweet, less chance of igniting a range war.* She settled into her sofa and drew her legs up under her.

"You been busy or somethin'?" he asked.

As if being engaged in meaningful work or some other engrossing and productive endeavor was beyond the range of possibilities, she thought.

Last she had heard Andrew was working part-time — very part-time — at a supermarket, stocking shelves. He was not exactly on the Nobel Prize track, she thought.

"I have been busy, yes. Between work and some spiritual adventures I'm on, it has been pretty exhausting."

"Whoa, spiritual adventures? That sounds pretty edgy for the mainstream princess, Jen. What kinda adventures we talkin' 'bout here?" He giggled, as though Jennifer had just let loose with an opening volley on the stage of The Improv.

"Well, Andrew, if you really want to know, I'm staring my sins against God in the face and trying to determine whether I want to have a blast on earth and spend eternity in Hell, or make up with the God who loves me despite myself and turn into a nun. Which do you think sounds right for me?"

Andrew was the ultimate postmodern, live-for-the-moment, damn-the-consequences-party-animal. Past efforts to discuss matters of faith with him had proven fruitless. He was probably not even aware that God exists.

There was a ten-second gap in the conversation while he processed what Jennifer had just said. Then he provided the prototypical retort.

"A nun?" he responded, incredulous. "But, like, yer not even Catholic. Doncha have to be Catholic to be a nun?"

Jennifer will always wonder how the gene pool works, producing the two of them from the same sources of sperms and eggs. "You're such a nitwit, Andrew. I'm not campaigning to be Mother Teresa's replacement. I'm just trying to figure out how to get right with God and convert my life from a meandering and ultimately meaningless voyage of frustration into a journey of purpose and joy."

"Huh? What's that mean, sis? Break it down."

"I think I've just been playing the role of a Christian, but I haven't really owned the part. I haven't truly embraced God as my soul mate for eternity."

"That's a play on words, right Jen? You know, like God's in the soul business, and you said He'd be your soul mate?"

Summoning a world-class act of will, Jennifer ignored the man with no brain and tried to complete her thoughts.

"I've been thinking through my life choices and have realized how infrequently I listen to God and follow His counsel. I've stunned myself at how infrequently I do things that I know will please Him, just to please Him. And realizing that about myself is crushing me, Andrew. I've realized that I am more in love with myself than with Him. I've been more worried about doing what makes me happy than doing what's right."

There was another long pause. Jennifer felt a doozy coming on.

"Wait, so you're saying there's something wrong with that?" he stuttered. "It's good to take care of yourself and have fun with others! You're so hard to talk to Jenny, I just don't know where you're comin' from."

"OK, Andrew, here's the bottom line. Yes, it's fine to love yourself, but not more than you love God. Sure, it's good to enjoy life and have fun with friends, but not if those activities conflict with God's values or replace Him at the center of your life. Yup, it makes sense to take care of yourself the best you can, but you have to recognize that your ultimate security is in God's hands, not yours."

"Well, yeah, I guess so. You're saying what I was thinking was right, aren't you?"

The conversation was getting nowhere. Jennifer figured there were ways to be a better steward of her time other than by talking to a stoner pantheistic narcissist, even if he was her brother. So she prepared to hang up.

"Andrew, let's just say this. My current preoccupation is allowing God to break my heart because of my adulterous affair with his adversary, and then to resuscitate that heart with His grace and hope. I'm not there yet, but I'm on a journey that has no end in sight, and I'm scared to death at the same time I'm getting more excited than I've ever been.

"You see, my life is becoming a walking contradiction, Andrew. I'm spiritually poor but eternally rich. Emotionally confused and drained but feeling energized by the incredible possibilities. I'm a smart person who makes a habit of doing dumb things."

Jennifer jumped up from the sofa, without giving Andrew time to formulate some sort of reply. "So, that's what's happenin' here, buck-aroo, thanks for callin', and I'll be in touch. Ciao!"

Demented goof-ball!

In the minutes after hanging up, Jennifer replayed her phone con-versation in her mind. She realized that how she had treated her poor misguided brother was exactly why she so desperately needed God to take control of her life.

APRIL 2, 11:32 A.M.

Dr. Neilsen stopped me in the hallway after the church service this week. I've been emailing back and forth with him about my journey. He has been so helpful. He asked how I was doing.

"You know how it is," I said, trying to hide my semi-depression from him. "Sometimes, I really hate that God lets me suffer like this."

"Oh, don't worry about that," he said nonchalantly, "You've caused God to suffer a lot more."

AT A CROSSROADS

Jennifer sat in bed on a Saturday night, wrapped in her flannel robe. A box of tissues was propped on a lump of bedclothes. Tears were leaking from the corners of her eyes. She reached for her cell phone.

She had been talking regularly by phone with Lauren since meet-ing her at Kevin and Kathy's. She had appreciated Lauren's wisdom and encouragement. Now she needed her strength.

Strength, and a sanity check. Of course, if I were really sane, I wouldn't expect an attractive, intelligent, wonderful single woman to be sitting home on a Saturday night!

"Hello?" Lauren answered on the third ring.

Maybe this is a sign that God isn't completely perturbed with me!

"Lauren? This is Jennifer."

"Hi Jennifer. What's going on?"

"I'm, uh, feeling a bit, uh, down. About my life. This sorrow thing is kicking in big time, and I'm feeling a little crazy..."

A sob escaped. Then another, she was sobbing into the receiver. *What a blubber bag I am!* "Sorry! I guess I'm feeling the weight of who I am...."

"Listen to me, Jennifer," Lauren nearly shouted over the intensifying wailing. "First of all, you're not going crazy, okay? I went back to some of the notes from a class I took during my time at your stage of the journey. It was a class about spiritual formation. They said it's normal that you move from understanding more about the journey to reaching a point when you need to purge yourself of all the garbage that has accumulated in your life. That's the brokenness we've been talking about. So this is normal, Jen! God is allowing you to feel some of the pain that you've subjected Him to over the years. Hurts, doesn't it?"

"Yeah — " That was all Jennifer could push through the tears and the aching that consumed her.

"That's great, Jennifer!"

Jennifer thought Lauren was exhibiting a bit more enthusiasm than she wanted to hear.

"After all, you are at a crossroads. You're either going to bust that shell around your heart and soul that has kept Him out, or you're going to be like most people and give in to the pain and hardship and just keep pretending you're a follower of Christ."

Jennifer sniffed and kept listening.

"The way I see it, Jennifer, you're on the precipice of graduating from being a typical follower of Jesus to be an accomplished imitator of Christ. I follow Chuck Colson, but that doesn't mean I do everything he does or says to do, or believe everything he writes or says. If I did, if I truly imitated him, that would make me a serious Colsonite, you know? It's the same way with Jesus. You can read about Him, say nice things about Him, go to good church events devoted to Him, and still not be a real imitator of Christ. Until you become a Christ clone, you're still playing on the periphery."

"A Christ clone?"

"Okay, that's a bit over the top," she admitted, "I made it up on the fly. But you see the point, don't you? Before you can be the bride of Christ — part of the living Church — you've got to deeply love Him and commit to Him. You've been engaged to Him for years but kept a lover on the side. Your distress is over the fact that you've finally made up your mind to be faithful to just one lover, and now you're smarting over how you've treated Him up to this point. That makes sense to me. Doesn't it make sense to you?"

"Yeah, but I've been such a jerk, so stupid and selfish, I'm almost too embarrassed to ask Him to stick it out with me."

"And that's why He's God and you're not, dorcas," she said playfully. "He can handle it. We're too soft, too wimpy, too sensitive, too hypocritical. But God gets it. Somehow, for reasons that still escape me, He set it all up this way, so that when we choose Him we *really* choose Him. When we decide to love Him, we really love Him. It's all good, girlfriend, it's all good. You're a celebration just waiting to happen."

"You really think so?" Jennifer whispered. She didn't feel like any kind of celebration she would want to be part of. She felt more like a funeral waiting to happen.

"Absolutely. This is part of the death-of-self we've been talking about. It's like you're attending your own funeral, and you're sad to see the old person die but happy because you know where they're going to wind up — right there with Jesus!"

Jennifer thought it was a little spooky that Lauren had picked up on the funeral-death-to-self connection. But she figured she understood the intellectual and emotional rollercoaster Jennifer had been riding for a couple of months, wrestling with the ins and outs, the ups and downs of this brokenness phase of the journey.

Jennifer thanked her and sent her a telephonic air kiss. "Good night, sister."

"Well, at least I'm not crazy. But I still feel like crap."

APRIL 17, 9:22 P.M.

I have always taken my commitments seriously. And now that I finally understood what God was asking me to commit to, the sheer magnitude of it took my breath away. Prompted by the Holy Spirit, I had initially made the emotional choice to love God with everything I have. But then I had to deal intellectually with the implications of that. I have been strategically studying the contours of this shift for weeks. And soon, I know, I'll have to convert the emotional and mental determination to love God fully with the proof: changing my lifestyle to reflect this total commitment to Him.

BROKEN WITH HOPE

Jennifer was in line at the Coffee Shack, head down, mulling over things.

"May I take your order?"

She looked up and realized the barista was addressing her. Then she realized the barista was Evan, the guy Lauren had mentioned as being another sojourner on the transformation trail. They had never formally met before, although they had shared a class or two, and attended a few of the same events. She couldn't help but stare for a moment.

"Miss?"

Suddenly she realized he was smiling at her, waiting for her order.

"Oh, yes. Um, I'll have a large latte, no whipped cream. And aren't you a friend of Lauren's?"

Turned out Evan said he was just about to take a dinner break, and suggested they go next door to the sandwich shop and talk for while. Jennifer felt awkward, especially since here was a good-looking single guy her age who loved Jesus, but she really wanted to hear what he had to say about the journey.

"So honestly, I'm in the midst of a kind of desperate search for peace with God, and I confess I'm willing to rope in anyone who can help," she said, laughing nervously.

"I know exactly what you mean," he said. "I've been there."

Evan gave Jennifer a thumbnail sketch of his own experience, and then asked her about how she viewed the role of faith in brokenness and restoration.

"Well, in this phase of the journey I've been so obsessed with understanding and dumping my sins that I've pretty much ignored the central place that faith must play in all of this," Jennifer acknowledged.

"Maybe it would help to remember Hebrews 11:6, which says that 'it is impossible to please God without faith. Anyone who wants to come to Him must believe that God exists and that He rewards those who sincerely seek Him.'"

"God gives you the seeds of faith," Evan reminded her as he took another bite of his tuna-veggie wrap. "You just have to nurture them and let them bear fruit. He wants to heal us. He wants to see the rift in our relationship with Him repaired as good as new. If we believe that He loves us that much, and we abandon ourselves to Him, then amazing things happen. But it all stems from having complete confidence in God: faith in His nature, His purposes, His power, His will, His Word, His grace, His guidance, and His blessings. He is always true to His promises."

Jennifer swished her latte around and watched the cinnamon swirl in a miniature whirlpool.

"That's pretty inspiring, Evan. And demanding, in terms of trust."

"Exactly. If your heart breaks over your sins against God, you then have to trust that He can wipe it all out and give you a clean slate."

"Yes, I know that intellectually, because that's the primary pitch evangelists use when speaking to nonbelievers. But having gone through the exercise of enumerating my countless sins over the course of my life — and I undoubtedly forgot or didn't even realize most of them — this idea of being broken with hope, the hope of total restoration and permanent love, is comforting. And motivating," Jennifer said, glancing up at Evan.

He was smiling. He had a nice smile.

As she drove home that evening, Jennifer thanked God that Evan turned out to be a very together guy, who laughed at the right places, showed sincere concern when it was merited, and offered some great advice.

And she thanked Him for the date she got out of the conversation, too. *Maybe this broken heart phase will wind up pretty good after all.*

MAY 24, 6:03 A.M.

I now have a much better understanding of what Jesus went through in the Garden of Gethsemane as He prayed to God. As His child, the Lord has endowed me with value, but the more introspective I get, the less I know what value that could possibly be, or why He would ever want a relationship with me. I am really struggling, feeling on the verge of depression as I recognize what kind of person I really am and then contrast that to the kind of Father He is. Sometimes I just want to die, but I know that's neither a viable way out nor the payoff to this journey.

Thankfully my friends who are farther down the path keep building me up, and I know they're praying for me, and God probably hears their prayers. I'm not so sure He hears mine. Why should He? What have I done to establish any credibility in His eyes or heart? More often than not these days I just feel miserable. This can't become a pity party. I have to pull myself together and get on the other side of this forlorn state. But when I look in the mirror now, I no longer see the same chipper, glowing, eager young woman who used to be there.

Now I see a selfish, mean-spirited, arrogant young American who has latched on to the term "Christian" because it was the best option available at the time. What a hypocrite! God has forgiven me and *loves* me? That would indeed be amazing, absolutely amazing grace.

JUNE 7, 4:23 P.M.

The Psalms have been a very helpful companion to me. I finally realized that throughout this portion of the journey I have been completely self-focused — and that that's been a lifelong condition (and problem). Jeremiah has been a good traveling companion too, reading about how his heart was broken and how God continued to provide him with perspective.

Oh Lord, give me the courage of these people who were after your own heart! Give me the love of Christ, the wisdom of Solomon, the perseverance of Paul, the courage of Joshua, the pragmatism of James, the honesty of Martha, and the capacity of Peter to be transformed.

I've been dwelling in the scriptures for a few weeks now, earnestly seeking what I need to be God's person on earth today. The Holy Spirit has given me new insights into so many of these passages, and allowed me to see the greater thread that runs across the lives and stories of these characters.

Thank God for the Bible! I understand how atheists can question its historicity and empirical veracity (hey, I went to college) but until you allow it to become a living guide to your personal journey, you cannot possibly grasp the priceless treasure God's words are for us.

And even so, this is the hardest thing I've ever done. But, as I'm starting to see, it may also be the only meaningful thing I've ever done. Have your way with me, Lord. I'm so over myself.

At least I think I am. That's probably an illusion, too. But at least I'm looking upward, to You, instead of always inward, to myself. That's got to be some progress, no?

JUNE 12, 7:02 A.M.

I may actually be gaining some ground on this journey. Three times in the last two days people at work have commented about how different I seem. Some of the adjectives they used — less stressed, more contemplative, quieter, gentler, less combative — may not be the kind of qualities that will get me a Fortune 500 CEO position. But they may demonstrate that at least the recalibrating over the past few months is grabbing hold of me.

But I do not sense that I have fully gleaned all that the Lord wants me to gain at this juncture of the journey. Strangely — or, at least, differently than before — I'm OK with that. My world is being redefined, and even though the process is painful — re-examining my collection of friends, use of money, lifestyle choices, church involvement, prayer focus, physical regimen, media habits, and more — I think it is proving to be a very positive, cleansing, hope-giving exercise.

Even my sense of my own future — what really matters, versus the success track I've pursued — seems to be changing. Every time I look at what the apostles Paul and Peter went through, I feel better about these very significant shifts in my perspective. I sense this is a vital part of the transformation process: purging the old, discovering and embracing the new.

CONNECTING WITH OTHERS

After church one day, Jennifer invited Doreen, the woman who serves as a spiritual director, to lunch. Over salads and ice tea, Jennifer shared with Doreen about her search for transformation.

Doreen, whose salt-and-pepper gray hair looked stylish in a

modern haircut, listened to everything Jennifer said with a slight smile and twinkling eyes.

"Jennifer," she said, when they had finished their meals, "I'm really happy to hear of your experiences. You have a long way to go, as we all do, but you've come so far."

She paused and gazed at Jennifer's face.

"And as we have talked about what you've been through and where you're headed, I'm struck by one thing that has not come up."

"What do you mean?" Jennifer asked, slightly apprehensive.

"You have described brokenness in terms of getting yourself right with God and being able to connect with Him at a deeper level. But I haven't heard you say anything about how the changes that come about through this experience will also impact how you connect with other people."

"Oh." Jennifer looked down at her empty salad plate, trying to think of how to respond.

"If your mind, heart and soul are redefined by this newfound depth of understanding and relationship, it should then impact how you relate to other people, too," Doreen continued. "If you become more loving toward God, that will facilitate the fruit of the Spirit. You remember Galatians 5:22-25, don't you?"

"Yes. Let's see: Love, joy, peace, patience, kindness, goodness, faithfulness, gentleness, and self-control," Jennifer recited.

"Yes. Embodying those qualities will naturally alter the relationships you have with people."

OCTOBER 1, 11:01 P.M.

"Everything else is worthless when compared to the value of knowing Christ Jesus my Lord. For His sake I have discarded everything else, counting it all as garbage, so that I could gain Christ and become one with Him. I no longer count on my own righteousness through obeying the law; rather, I become righteous through faith in Christ."

That's Philippians 3:7-9. I'm ready to move on from this stop on the journey. That verse expresses what I want: to abandon all the worthless things that have ruled my life and instead devote myself to knowing and loving God. I realize that the tough times are not over in my journey, but now I am excited to struggle and suffer through them because I want to turn myself over to God in the fullest way possible.

John 15:5 has become a constant companion, too, where Jesus tells us, "Apart from me, you can do nothing." He reminds us that we will not get the journey right without the powerful touch and guidance of our creator. So I am officially done playing God in my life. Besides, I was pretty bad at it.

I know now, beyond a shadow of doubt, that I want nothing more and nothing less than a full, loving relationship with God. I am sad that I have wasted literally years of time that could have been spent knowing Him and being closer to Him, serving Him better and becoming the woman who thrills Him. But at least I'm on that pathway now. Better late than never.

Onward on the journey. And unlike the subject in the famous U2 song, I think I'm about to find what I've been looking for...

CHAPTER 9

APPROACHING INTEGRATION

MARCH 5, 7:03 A.M.

Looking back over the last four or so years, I am amazed at how my life has been transformed. I hardly recognize myself!

Remember those early naïve questions when I was so restless with Christianity? How far God has brought me! Of course, I now realize I have even further to go than when I started the journey! I have met amazing people and had incredible experiences on this journey to spiritual maturity. But I will be the first to admit that we never achieve total maturity!

(And if I ever get to a point where I claim that final goal, you'll know I have deceived myself and failed in my quest to be all that God made me to be. God forbid that I should ever become so deluded and complacent!)

Here's one of the biggest insights I've gleaned. It's certainly the most challenging aspect of the journey to date. Genuine transformation requires growth in all four dimensions of my being — <u>mind, heart, body and spirit</u> — simultaneously!

If I advance in faith intellectually but not emotionally, then I fail to reach full maturity.

If I grow emotionally but don't put those faith-driven feelings physically into practice, my faith is incomplete and unproductive.

If I do good works in the name of the Lord but do so based on my own ambition rather than the guidance and power of the Holy Spirit, I have done admirable but empty deeds.

If I connect with God deeply but am unable to help others experience that same depth of relationship with Him, I have simply been a selfish person.

This notion runs parallel to 1 Corinthians 13, doesn't it? In the famous "love chapter," Paul writes about the necessity of loving God and people through our gifts and abilities. In fact, his words emphasize that doing all the things that the world recognizes as special — for example, speaking multiple languages fluently, accurately foretelling the future, knowing God's "secret plans," having unshakeable faith, giving everything away to help the poor, sacrificing your body for a higher purpose — is meaningless unless we give real love to others.

Likewise, the supernatural gifts God provides to us are meaningless unless they are used in the context of loving God and people. I love Paul's passionate plea: "Three things will last forever — faith, hope and love — and the greatest of these is love. Let love be your highest goal." [15]

I now believe transformation is simpler — conceptually — than many theologians have made it out to be.

Our fallen world promotes self-love more than God-love or other-love. That's what makes transformation so hard. Because transformation is nothing more and nothing less than loving God and people more than yourself.

APRIL 2, 8:23 P.M.

One of my most humbling insights through this journey has been that I speak about love all the time, but don't really understand what love is!

I suspect that most people are this way. We have become so surrounded by talk about love that it has ceased to have meaning.

So a significant objective of this portion of my journey has been to get a grip on what love is. Yes, I can quote the usual definitions, and even cite the most common Greek words used in scripture for love (agape, philia, eros). But truly comprehending the nature of love is a different matter!

I think the journey has been slowed down by the need to grasp this concept. But I'd rather slow down and make sustainable progress than blast forward only to have to retreat later (when my shallowness is revealed!).

So back to those four dimensions! Thanks to a lot of time thinking about it and debating it with my friends and mentors, I've decided that I need to allow God to integrate my mind, heart, body and spirit. That's the only way for me to become a more complete and mature follower of Christ.

Jesus may well have been the only human being ever to achieve a perfect integration of love within each of these dimensions. But every one of us has been commissioned with the privilege of imitating Christ in all of His aspects! So, it's clear to me that integration is the means to becoming the ultimate Jennifer — the woman that God sees in me!

JUNE 12, 2:02 P.M.

Back to thinking about integration. I've been collecting some conclusions regarding practices that are integral to becoming a transformed disciple of Jesus. Here are some:

- You cannot overcome fears and anxieties (matters of the heart) without prayer (a practice of the spirit).

- You cannot feel truly grateful (a matter of the heart) unless you understand truth, grace, and holiness (matters of the mind).

- You cannot express forgiveness (a matter of the heart) without healing words and supportive behavior (matters of the body).

- You cannot understand faith (a matter of the mind) without giving the Holy Spirit the opportunity to influence your thinking (a matter of spirit).

- You cannot interpret the scriptures accurately (a matter of the mind) without personal experience (a matter of the body).

- You cannot discern God's will (a matter of the mind) without experiencing His love (a matter of the heart).

- You cannot truly repent (which affects all four dimensions) unless you experience a broken heart (a matter of the heart), a decision to change (a matter of the mind), a commitment to new behaviors (a matter of the body) and an invitation to the Holy Spirit to empower such change (a matter of the spirit).

- You cannot release the Holy Spirit in your life (a matter of the spirit) until you subjugate your ego (a matter of the heart), accept your inferiority to God (a matter of the mind), and alter your life practices (a matter of the body).

You know what else? Repentance is something that never ends. The more I understand, and feel, and experience, and allow God to reveal, the more robust my repentance becomes.

Similarly, the more complete my dependence on God becomes, the more possible it has been for me to have faith in Him, to accept other people for who they are, and to engage in acts of kindness without feeling as if I am doing something special that deserves recognition or reward.

Remember what Henri Nouwen wrote? He said life is "a short opportunity for us to tell God that we love Him."

And we can't just tell God we love Him. We need to express it through all four dimensions.

So I have been meditating on how I can share my love for God through my feelings; through my understanding of Him and the world He has created; through the ways I love people as a reflection of my love for Him; and by allowing the Holy Spirit to speak to God on behalf with words that transcend human comprehension and expression.

STANDING STRONG

It was nearly closing time. Jennifer sipped on her latte and glanced around The Coffee Shack. She felt a little alone.

She glanced down at her journal. Flipping back two years through the pages, she landed on November 3, the entry where she recorded the sad news that her dear spiritual advisor Doreen had passed away. It had been unexpected. "This is a big blow to me," Jennifer had written. "Doreen really 'got it' and was such a gentle and helpful advisor to me. I'm going to miss her terribly."

She did. In fact, in these few recent years there had been other enormous relational changes in her life. Evan, the handsome and fun barista, moved out of state, accepting an opportunity to work with disadvantaged children in an inner-city setting.

"I know he'll be great at it, and his enthusiasm about the work drips off the emails he sends me," Jennifer had written.

Pastor Brian was hired by a church across the country and was loving his new group of people. Even Olivia, who headed Jennifer's church's prayer ministry, wound up leaving when her husband was offered a major promotion overseas. "I know she desperately misses her friends, but I also know that she'll adjust well because she still has her closest friend with her, just a prayer away," Jennifer had jotted down.

Thank goodness I'm still in touch with Kevin and Kathy, and with Dr. Neilsen, she thought.

But, sitting alone in her favorite spot in the coffee house, she realized that although her circle of spiritual confidantes had contracted, and she was sad at seeing friends depart, she felt undeniably strong and capable without them.

She fired up her netbook started an email note to Wil Neilsen.

PROFOUNDLY LOVING

"So what do you think the ultimate sign of transformation is?"

Jennifer was back in Dr. Neilsen's office, in that familiar old comfy chair facing his oak desk on a beautiful autumn day.

"Yup, that's the big question, isn't it? Kind of like, 'what's the meaning of life'?" he snickered, flashing a grin.

"But it's a legitimate question, isn't it? I mean, if we can't answer it, how are we going to experience it?"

"No, I'm not denying the legitimacy of the question. I'm simply reacting to the fact that few people seem to ever get to the end of that rainbow."

He paused, leaned over to the edge of his desk and took a handful of peanuts from the bowl he keeps there. He munched on them for a minute or so, peering out his office window. He turned back to Jennifer.

"I read somewhere that we make Christianity way too complex, almost like the Pharisees did with Judaism, laying all of their rules and routines on the Jewish people," he began. "The essence of Christianity is very simple, of course: love God fully, and love people the same way. Everything in Jesus's teaching points to those two expressions as the crux of His model and mission. So I guess I'd argue that the most foolproof sign of transformation is profoundly loving God and people."

The two already had had a lively discussion about the role of the four life dimensions in the transformation process.

"And what makes our love 'profound' is the ability to love God and others with all of our heart, our mind, our behavior and our spirit, right? It seems like few people ever achieve that goal," Wil said, shaking his head.

Some people get far enough along the path that they get good at loving in an intellectual way, he said. They understand love, they concur about its goodness, they can identify when it happens and even the conditions under which love is appropriate or most difficult.

"But despite that knowledge about love, such love is absent in their lives in terms of their emotions, their actions or their spirituality. They experience a degree of transformation, yes, but they never really get to the end of the path and know the fullness of life that Christ intends them."

Jennifer nodded. She was thinking of a few friends in that category.

"For other people," Wil continued, "the obstacle is getting beyond emotional mastery of love, or behavioral mastery, or a faith-focused love fest. None of that is bad, and it's a necessary component of achieving profundity in love, but it's unfortunate that most people do not experience the complete package that's available."

"I know what you're saying, but why don't we experience the full journey?" Jennifer asked. "These are good people and they have made an incredible effort to allow God to reshape them into a better person, a more Christ-like person. What's the real hang-up? Why won't God allow them to make it to the end of the journey?"

Again, Wil gazed out the window, wearing a sad smile. "I don't know."

He ran his hands through his short, graying hair. "Perhaps it's because we just cannot seem to fully cooperate with God. We make some dimensions of our life unavailable to Him. It's probably not intentional, it's just a natural barrier that we erect in response to any attempt to take us beyond our comfort zone in those areas of our life."

He gave a quick chuckle. "I don't know about you, but I can sure relate to that struggle!"

Jennifer smiled. "Yep. Me too. What else, do you think?"

"Well, here's a thought. Perhaps it's because He is holding out some of the best for our transition to the next life, when we can love Him with perfection in Heaven."

Jennifer held his gaze and nodded. Dr. Neilsen's thoughtful analysis had confirmed her suspicions about what she faced in these final stops on the journey.

"I am unexpectedly content with where my life is at now, Wil. I know I have a lot of room for growth. But I'm satisfied that I'm on the right path and continuing to make progress. Transformation, I've learned, isn't a program that you attack and complete, clear about when you have reached the end of the process. It isn't a task that has a definable beginning and end. It's an open-ended expedition with the ultimate tour guide, a new adventure every day, a pilgrimage that continues forever. If you can get over the need to have tangible closure, it's actually pretty invigorating."

FOCUSING ON THE LOVE OF GOD

Jennifer's front door rattled. Someone wasn't just knocking; the visitor was making a statement.

"Andrew! Just come in! Leave the door on its hinges, for heaven's sake," Jennifer yelled.

Her brother has been stopping by her apartment on a regular basis lately. A few years ago that would have been unthinkable. But now, the wayward son apparently had begun thinking more seriously about be-

120

coming a productive member of society. Surprising to Jennifer, he also had been tentatively bringing up faith matters.

Back again. I guess it just proves that you can never give up on anyone's soul. Perhaps my prayers will pay off yet, she thought as she headed for the front room.

This being Saturday, and Andrew still working only part-time jobs despite his prolonged search for "a real job," his presence wasn't entirely unexpected. She hugged her younger bro, who towered over her. He headed for the kitchen.

After raiding the refrigerator and pantry, Andrew settled in at the kitchen table with an armload of food. After a few minutes of light banter he surprised her by asking, "So, uh, how's that love quest thing you're doing? Getting anywhere?"

Has he run out of conversation nuggets so quickly? she wondered. But she was happy to fill him in on her latest spiritual meanderings.

He chomped around a ham sandwich. "Seems to me that if the deal is figuring out how to love God and people, you're better off putting people on hold and putting your attention on the Big Man," he opined.

"I'm not sure I have that option, Andrew. Love is not an either-or option. I don't get to choose whether or not to love, and I don't get to choose who I'd rather love. I'm called — all of us are called — to love both God and *every* human being, even you, bro. The challenge for me has been — "

"No, sis, that's not my point," he interrupted, raising the hand that didn't hold a fistful of tortilla chips. "What I'm saying is, you probably can't break the love code on both God and people simultaneously, so it makes more sense to put your coin on the Guy Upstairs."

"Okay, why?"

"Shoot, think about it, Jen. You got two possibilities here. You can love the divine presence that supposedly loves you. Or you can love a bunch of nutcases that run around the planet trying to outdo each other. Doesn't seem that hard to figure out who's gonna be easier to love, your God or the creatures He made. If I were in your shoes I'd put the target on the G-Man first and once you have that squared away, maybe He'd help you figure out how to love the rest of us."

OCTOBER 3, 7:32 P.M.

I have to confess, I was stunned at what Andrew said this afternoon.

How had my beach bum of a scatterbrained brother recognized my priority before I did?

After he left to go who-knows-where, I snuggled into my easy chair and pondered his contention. It made sense. Sure, I must love both God and people, but in all likelihood I will get there with God first.

Even the scriptures seem to intimate that I cannot fully love people until I first discover how to love the One who loved me first and completely. In fact, the Bible suggests that all I'm really doing is giving the overflow of God's love that He's given to me, to other people. Loving God is the easier of the two challenges, and strategically the smartest. Duh!

Now that I think about it, those fellow believers on the journey who seem to be at the "profound love" stage, do indeed appear to have figured out how to love God before they reached a place where they had extreme love for humanity. Why would I be any different?!

God once spoke through a donkey. So why couldn't He choose to help me get my priorities straight by communicating through a contemporary nomad?

CHAPTER 10

UNDERSTANDING LOVE: ALIGNING THE MIND

NOVEMBER 8, 10:01 P.M.

For quite some time now I have been wrestling with several concepts in 1 John 4. Here are the primary instigators of my struggle:

- "Love comes from God." (verse 7)

- "God is love, and all who live in love live in God, and God lives in them. As we live in God, our loves becomes more perfect." (verses 16-17)

- "If we don't love people, whom we can see, how can we love God, whom we cannot see?" (verse 20)

Okay, one, it seems as if scripture teaches that if we truly have accepted God as our Father and Christ as our savior, then He lives within us, through His Holy Spirit.

Two, the presence of the Spirit allows us to return the love of God that is in us back to God. Just as we are not responsible for receiving salvation, this love we give Him is not something we have manufactured but merely reflects our willingness to allow God to determine how we live.

Three, He wants us to love Him, He has given us the divine means of doing so, therefore it is a question of whether we will allow Him to receive back the gift of love He first gave to us.

Four, by the same token, He has provided us with the capacity to love other people, and we do not completely love God until we love other people, too.

All of this has been a revelation to me — a disheartening one!

Jesus reminded us that the world hated Him first (John 15:18), a theme picked up by Paul (Romans 5:10, Colossians 1:21). But I had never stopped to consider that we remain hostile towards Him until our hearts are broken and we surrender everything and submit to His will and His ways.

Further, as I have thought about the integration of love across all four dimensions of my life, my limitations have become even more obvious.

After some serious soul searching, it became apparent that my natural tendency, honed over more than thirty years of practice, has been to lead with my mind and follow through with my body, while ignoring my heart and soul as much as possible.

As I have attempted to fabricate the love that I offered to Him and others, God's love has had little to with it! My friends have enabled me to see that until I better understand His love and get all four of these cylinders firing in synch, my ability to fully love God and people will be hindered, despite making huge progress related to surrendering my life to God.

So these last few months have been mostly devoted to gaining insight into how to reach the place where I would have, in Dr. Neilsen's words, "profound love." To ease into it, I have started with an exploration of how to express love and facilitate the expression of love through my mind.

I've narrowed my exploration to four basic elements:

- Understanding what love is.
- Identifying the times when I have experienced love.
- Imagining the times when I must give love.
- Figuring out how to give love.

It's not quite that simple, of course, but I decided I had to examine those four general areas before I could have a sufficient grasp of loving God and people with my entire mind.

It has been said that the Bible is God's love letter to His people. Although many pastors, preachers and teachers focus primarily on Jesus's death and resurrection as the supreme act of love, the scriptures have love lessons littered through them from Genesis through Revelation.

Not only is love the unifying theme throughout the scriptural narrative; love is, in Paul Tillich's observation, the great unifying power that influences our existence.

God loved us first, and not because we deserved His love. We have not been given His love because we are worthy — having His love gives us worth.

WHAT IS LOVE?

From the moment Jennifer juggled her infamous strawberry cheesecake in one hand and rang Kevin and Kathy's doorbell with the other to her departure nearly at midnight, the evening with her old friends was fun, stimulating and full of joy.

"It's been too long!" Kathy cried, as she welcomed Jennifer into their warm home. A smiling Kevin gave her a big hug, and motioned her toward the kitchen.

As always, Kevin and Kathy were gracious hosts. The three enjoyed a delicious homemade meal and laughed until their sides hurt, telling stories of the silliest moments they'd ever experienced. Then, calmer and with coffee mugs in hand, they moved into the family room and commandeered the comfortable chairs.

"Well, you probably won't be surprised that I've been thinking of a few things lately I want to ask you about," Jennifer started. "I've been reading a lot lately, trying to get a better understanding of what love is."

"That's our Jennifer, doing her homework and then thinking it through until everything is in its proper place," laughed Kathy.

"Tell us what you've been reading," Kevin asked. Jennifer mentioned the range of sources she'd consulted, from psychologists like Erich Fromm to pastors as disparate as Charles Stanley and John Wesley.

"Great stuff. But let's start with the Bible. I know you've examined it for answers too." he said. "In particular, let's look at two passages I know you've considered — 1 Corinthians 13 and Galatians 5."

He asked Kathy to read aloud the famous "love chapter," and Jennifer to read the well-known "fruit of the spirit" passage.

"Now take a look at the words Paul wrote to the Corinthians. It helped me understand his message there by translating the negative into positives. If you do that, one way we might read about love is to see that it is kind, reasonable, humble, respectful, accommodating, peaceful, forgiving, good, diligent, faithful, and hopeful," he stated while following Paul's words in his Bible with his index finger under each word. "And now, if you look at the Galatians section, we might say that list includes loving, joyful, peaceful, patient, kind, good, faithful, gentle, self-controlled, reasonable, humble, repentant, and Spirit-led."

He paused for a minute, flipping back and forth between the two passages, then looked up and asked us, "So what do these two passages talk about?"

"Well, the safe answer is love," Jennifer said tenuously.

"Yes, but what else do they share?" he continued. "What are all these qualities of?"

After a few moments of staring at the Bibles they held, Kathy suggested, "They're all aspects of our personality and demeanor."

"Yes, that's my reckoning, too," Kevin responded. "Do you notice how much overlap there is between the two sections?"

He pointed out the attributes patient, kind, reasonable, humble, peaceful and faithful. Then he said one could argue that the term "self-controlled" in Galatians 5 encompasses the terms respectful and accommodating — or, "not rude and not demanding its own way" — in the Corinthians passage.

"So, to a significant extent, these passages are complementary. They describe the reality of what it means to be loving."

He reached for his mug. "And one of the keys to it all is in Galatians 5:25, where it reminds us that we are to be 'living by the Spirit' and supposed to 'follow the leading of the Spirit in every part of our lives.' That goes back to your quest for integration, Jennifer, but also emphasizes

WHAT IS LOVE?	
1 Corinthians 13:1-13	**Galatians 5:22-25**
Patient	Patience
Kind	Kindness
Reasonable (not jealous)	Reasonable (not jealous)
Humble (not boastful or proud)	Humble (not conceited)
Peaceful (not irritable)	Peace (not provoking)
Good (dislikes injustice, loves truth)	Goodness
Faithful (never loses faith)	Faithfulness
Respectful (not rude)	Self-control
Accommodating (not demand its own way)	Gentleness
Forgiving (keeps no record of being wronged)	Forgiven/Repentant (nailed passions and desires to the cross)
Diligent (never gives up, endures)	Spirit-driven (live by, follow Spirit's leading)
Hopeful	Joy

the fact that we cannot do this on our own. It must be driven by God's Holy Spirit who lives within us. And that, I think, goes back to the process of surrendering and submitting."

"Kevin, I'd like to know what Jennifer has learned about how to align our minds with God's." She beamed her 100-megawatt smile at Jennifer.

Jennifer paused, as if trying to decide where to start.

"I've come to believe that loving God starts with faith," she began. She was very aware that these two people were further along on their journey than she, and she hoped her approach to learning — studying and analyzing information, aided by prayer — was adequate to shed some light on how to love God and others through our mind.

"I'm thinking of Hebrews 11, verse one, where it talks about faith. It describes it as something that gives us confidence, even though there's not much 'hard evidence' of what we hope for and believe in. My faith is unshakeable at this point because I fully trust in God's love, which He has demonstrated to me over and over again, and I see Him giving that same love to others who pursue Him, too. He has an unblemished track record. That bolsters my confidence, too. And I have come to lean on Jesus's words to His disciples in Matthew 19, when He announced that with God, everything is possible. I believe that although it is a matter of informed faith."

Kevin slapped his knee, and grinned at me and burst forth with a hearty, "Here, here!" Jennifer smiled. "But aligning my mind with God so that I can love Him takes more than just faith," she continued. "It's imperative that we become students of the scriptures, so that our minds line up with His perspective."

She placed her hand on the Bible in her lap. "A significant purpose for knowing the Bible inside and out is to better understand His will for me, not just in grand ways but in every circumstance of every day. Sometimes that sense of direction comes through prayer, but even then my interpretation must be consistent with His principles and history, which requires me to be conversant with His word."

"So true, Jennifer," Kathy said. "And so important out in the world."

"Yes, I realize that for all of this to work, I have to be alert at all times. Alert to His presence. Alert to signs He provides. Alert to danger that lurks in every situation. Alert to opportunities He offers. And oddly," she grinned, "that same alertness should also produce a slower decision-making cycle for me because I need time to take everything to God and wait on Him for the appropriate direction."

She said she no longer operated independent of anyone else. "Now it's Jennifer and God, with Jennifer the recipient of God's direction and in charge of executing His judgments rather than making and implementing my own. If my life is really His, then my choices must be, too."

"That must have produced a big shift in your lifestyle, Jennifer," said Kevin.

"It sure has. People at work aren't sure what to make of it. But they've learned to roll with it, especially since they've seen some pretty amazing results."

"Well, I'm impressed," Kevin said, taking another slug of coffee. "And here's one more element to add to the mix."

Kevin described how it felt important to acknowledge the reality of God's love. He said this may be accomplished by identifying His acts of love, by taking advantage of the opportunities given to love others on His behalf, and by recognizing limitations and weaknesses when it comes to loving people.

"When I understand love at that level, I've found it reduces, if not eliminates, uncertainty in addressing people and situations. This is that 'God consciousness' we have talked about — being aware of God's presence and availability every waking moment. One theologian referred to it as acknowledging God's 'habitual presence.'"

Kathy had been relatively quiet during our chat, but now she jumped in. "Maybe part of the mental commitment to love is that we see this as part of our Christian duty. This is our assignment from God. It's no more an option for our survival than eating or sleeping is."

"Could you elaborate, Kathy? I'm a bit wary of adopting a legalist perspective," said Jennifer. "You know — 'I love God because I have to' attitude."

"Sure. Jesus told us, when He described the greatest commandments, that we are supposed to love Him and others with our whole mind. In John 13, and then again in first John four, the apostle quoted Jesus as telling us to love each other because God loved us first. And Peter talked to the disciples about truth and the results we experience from obeying God, which should motivate us to love Him."

Kevin put down his mug and picked up where his wife left off.

"I've always found John's gospel and epistles to be fascinating. On the one hand, we associate him with being the disciple of love, the one who gushes emotionally about what love means. But if you read John more carefully, you'll find that while John does call for love, it's not about emotionalism."

He picked up his Bible. "I think it's in John 14, verse 15, where he quotes Jesus as saying, 'If you love me, obey my commandments.' Yes, here."

He looked up and smiled. "Very simple. Most commentators and preachers seem to interpret that as an emotional challenge, but obedience is not about emotion. It is more of a condition of the mind and spirit. You don't defeat sin based on emotion alone. Often, it starts with a prompting in your spirit, followed by your mind making a determined choice to act in a given way, one that denies the power of sin because you can see the negative consequences."

Kathy stood. "Well, I can see some negative consequences if we don't take a break. Jennifer, feel free to visit the guest bathroom, if you need to, while I go make a fresh pot of coffee."

DECEMBER 9, 8:02 A.M.

Last night was amazing. By the end of our three-hour discussion (to almost midnight!), I was mentally drained!

I left Kevin and Kathy's house more convinced than ever that authentic love of God is not solely about reining in the mind and aligning it with God — but it's not possible without that alignment.

I had apologized to them for talking about love as if it could be compartmentalized into separate but equal mind, heart, behavior and spirit areas. I just needed to get a grip on it that way.

I shared how I first have been trying to understand the intellectual aspects of how to love. A combination of scriptural wisdom and my own experiences point to the fact that to love God and others demands a commitment to placing them first, forgiving any issues that may have come between us, and working toward having a sincere appreciation and affection for them. Loving others means that I have to give them part of me.

Kevin asked what that meant in practical terms. Good question! I said for one thing, it means making my personal agenda secondary. God's will is that I love Him first, others second, myself third.

Of course, that means overlooking a lot of hurtful things people say or actions they take. I can't be foolish enough to invite continued pain, but I have to be willing to forgive them after we discuss those matters.

It also means seeking harmony with everyone, which sounds like one of those ridiculous politically correct ideals, but it becomes a practical, Spirit-driven reality if I look for ways to support, encourage and help others (without necessarily endorsing some of their inappropriate or even ungodly ideas and behaviors). Jesus calls us to be servants, so I've been working at figuring out how to serve people without denying God's truths and principles.

"Would you say, then, that love cannot be given until you develop a new attitude toward God and people?" Kevin asked.

I hadn't thought of it on those terms, but that was exactly what I was thinking. He said it had taken him a long time to understand that, and the attitude had to come from God. Then he said something very memorable. I am paraphrasing but I think this is the essence:

"I had fooled myself into thinking that my attitude toward God and people was just fine, when in fact it needed a significant adjustment. One of the things that helped me fine-tune my attitude was not figuring out how to love people, but why I should do so. Kathy alluded to some of the reasons earlier, but I also discovered that I owe love because I am called to imitate Jesus. I am blown away by God's forgiveness, which motivates me to forget all my pettiness and competitiveness and just love; and because if Jesus sees goodness in these people, I should, too. All of those were factors in my being able to get my head around what love is, why to love, and how to do it."

I know that I am on the path toward achieving that convergence, but last night's discussion has challenged me in some new ways that undoubtedly will refine my mind for God.

CHAPTER 11

FEELING THE LOVE: ALIGNING THE HEART

FEBRUARY 14, 10:12 A.M.

One of the quirks of my personality is that I have never been a real ooey-gooey emotional person, like women are usually expected to be. I have feelings, of course, but I'm not always driven by them, or even aware of them. My intellect usually overwhelms my emotion, which is probably what has made the integration of love throughout all four dimensions of my being such a challenge.

To help me make greater sense of this aspect of love, I enlisted the aid of my long-time girlfriend Lauren. Cancer-free for nearly a decade now, Lauren has been my most reliable partner on this trek toward wholeness. She is more dominant in the emotional area than the mental dimension although she's a smart cookie! We've had the opportunity to help each other, by my describing what I've learned about syncing my mind with God, while she has been coaching me in relation to aligning my heart with Him.

MANAGING EMOTIONS

Lauren slid into the restaurant booth with a smile on her broad, dark face. She was wearing new designer eyeglasses, and had her hair in shoulder-length braids.

"Whoa, aren't you looking good, sista!" Jennifer joked.

"You know it, girl!" Lauren laughed. They teased each other about their ethnic differences. "I'm feeling good too!"

"Well, that's just what I wanted to talk about!" Jennifer said as she popped open the menu.

After they ordered, Jennifer explained what she had been learning about aligning the four areas of her self with God, including the heart. She asked for advice in the realm of emotions.

"Well, when you get right down to it," Lauren began, nibbling nachos from the plate of appetizers, "feeling the love of God and incorporating it into who you are is a bit of a paradox."

"What do you mean?" Jennifer asked, grabbing a buffalo wing.

"For instance, I've found that accepting God's love means I can be fearless. After all, what do I have to fear if He loves me and keeps His promises to me? But at the same time, love means forgiving those who hurt me or let me down. So I know that simply loving God is not going to be simple!"

Jennifer smiled and nodded, licking sauce off her fingers. "And we're supposed to be overtaken by a sense of joy and peacefulness, at the same time we're in the world experiencing hardships and persecution," Jennifer said. "I keep thinking of King David's life. He was the guy who the Bible says had a heart similar to God's, and his life hardly was marked by serenity and celebration!"

"You're right. All of that moved me to try to recalibrate the basis of my emotions," Lauren said. "Instead of allowing my emotions free rein, I have tried to take control over them and … manage them, I guess is how I'd describe it."

Jennifer asked her to give some details about what that looked like.

"Joy is a good example. The Bible says that our joy is a result of receiving God's love, and that we ought to be joyful people. I used to equate that with happiness, which in turn relates to how I felt about my circumstances. But that's wrong. Joy is a deeper sense of well-being that's caused by being in the presence and good graces of God."

Her sense of purpose and significance was grounded not in who she is or what she accomplishes — "or how I feel" — but in the fact that God Himself knows her and cares about her.

"He loves us, Jennifer! If we truly get that, it should produce a sense of joy, don't you think?"

They shared a laugh at how simple some of the transformational process is — and how complicated people can make it.

"I will say," Jennifer offered, wondering if this might be her only contribution to the discussion, "that a similar line of reasoning has helped me to feel a deeper peace with God in the past year or so. As you say, knowing that God has my back in any situation that arises has relieved my worries about outcomes. And you know me, I'm all about outcomes. But I've come to realize that while outcomes do matter — to me and also to God — His love is so complete and undeniable that it puts a wall of protection around my heart. If I can remember to share the moment with God — doing my part, of course — then He will take care of it. It puts me at ease — alert, but not worried or fearful."

The waiter brought their orders.

"One of the things you said has been really important for me," Lauren noted. "Letting God take care of things does not mean that I will get my way. Or that I will not face harsh situations. But that's not because God isn't listening to my prayers, or that He loves others more than me. It's simply part of how He is maturing me. That's love: allowing me to experience some of the pain we've thrown His way, but using it strategically to help me grow up."

Jennifer stirred her ice tea and thought for a moment.

"I guess He has impacted my heart more than I've realized," she said, looking around the restaurant. "The more I have understood His love — there goes my mind again, the wheels always turning — the more my heart has relaxed."

Lauren was nodding. "Uh huh. And...?"

"Well, I guess I could describe it as adopting a deeper, well, humility, given the depth and breadth of His love for me. And that, in turn, has sparked a genuine gratitude, a kind of love that has caused me to feel differently toward God, yes, but even more so toward other people."

She realized that she had arrived at the place where she was seeing more clearly God's sacrifice for her, and accepting other people as He had accepted her.

"That means not even looking at all the garbage that takes place between people, but focusing instead on the goodness in them, the potential they represent, the fact that God made them and loves them just as He does with me, and my obligation to them, because of God's love, is to pass on the love He gives me so willingly and abundantly."

The two women sat in silence for a few moments as they chewed on the truths they had put into words, and chewed on their meal.

"But you know that all of this comes back to faith, right?" Lauren said. "I mean, without a profound trust and confidence in God, without a pervasive awareness of who He is and what He has done to save us and build us up — without all that, such a heartfelt love in not even imaginable. So, in some ways, it all comes back to having authentic and unshakeable faith."

MARCH 14, 6:31 P.M.

This must be a test from God. At work, Thom has been spreading really ugly rumors about my sexuality, telling lies about my finances, making fun of my beliefs, publicly questioning whether I add any value to what we produce, setting me up for confrontations in group meetings, attributing errors to me that I had nothing to do with — it's awful!

Why has he chosen me as his enemy? It's a full-on attack. It makes no sense. We've never butted heads before. We've worked well on past projects, and I've always gone out of my way to give him credit and thanks for his efforts. Does he covet my job? Is he struggling with his wife? (She's an executive at a major financial institution, probably makes triple what Thom makes — so now he's got it out for all women executives?) Or is this just a side of him I never noticed because I was too busy climbing the corporate ladder and only now have the eyes to see what a weasel he is? (Lord, is it okay for me to call him a weasel? He really is, you know? Are You at least chuckling, Lord?)

The pain I feel is real. Where is my BFF, my savior, my confidante, to take it away? Why haven't You protected me? Do I really have to learn whatever this lesson is by going through this hurt?

The biggest hardship for me, though, is trying to love my "enemy." How can I love the guy who each day eagerly comes to work to stick a bigger knife in my back? Turn the other cheek? Forgive? Be grateful for tribulations? Are you kidding me? My natural instinct is to develop a plan and crush this bully, absolutely lacerate this snake to ribbons. I wouldn't call it revenge; I'd call it justice.

But I know that's wrong, that's the old Jennifer. The new Jennifer is not expected to be a pushover or a pansy — yes, I need to respond and even anticipate Thom's inappropriate behavior — but even more so, I need to love him. God says so in His word, and in my heart I know that's the right thing to do.

Romans 12:17-18 calls me to "do things in such a way that everyone can see [I am] honorable. Do all [I] can to live in peace with everyone." And in 1 Thessalonians 5:15, Paul writes that we should "always try to do good to each other and to other people." I sure wish he had added, "whenever it is easy or comfortable do so." Maybe he forgot?

If love is as powerful as I have come to believe, then love will get me through this. And it might even restore Thom to a better place. Scripturally I know the process starts with forgiveness, and I'm working on that. (I guess I'm not as mature as I thought I was; probably hadn't been sufficiently tested to show how far I've come and how far I have to go.)

Starting today, I am following the directive in Matthew 5:44: I am now praying for God's blessings upon Thom. And I am praying that God will renew my heart in this process, giving me a deeper capacity to love, forgive be grateful, and experience the joy of knowing God and knowing that I am blameless in this situation. I am also praying that Luke 6:35-36 will be my way: doing good to Thom, giving him what he doesn't deserve, being compassionate toward him. Oh, man, how will I accomplish this?

Stupid question. The answer is only through the power of the Holy Spirit working through a submitted Jennifer.

Lord, help me become the loving person you see within me. Then perhaps we can move on to healing, restoration and reconciliation.

That road to recovery looks mighty long and tough from where I'm standing now.

But traveling that road must be my commitment. Transformation is never easy, and this is more proof of it for me. It's also a reminder that I'm still on the journey, and need to continue working at converting what I know (via my mind) into how I feel (through my heart) as expressed through words and actions (from my body) that coincide with the guidance of the Holy Spirit (via my soul). That's the kind of integration I've been striving to experience. Perhaps this skirmish with Thom is simply God giving me a chance to blend the four dimensions of love in a practical way.

MAY 31, 2:12 P.M.

Although Evan moved away, we have remained in touch through various means of communication. I even received a letter — does anyone send letters via snail mail anymore? — the other day. He wrote about various topics, but one section of his note resonated with me. He has been having his own struggles regarding love and pain, based on issues he has with his family that have affected how he sees God and other people (especially women, as it turns out). Here is part of what he wrote:

> Granted, God wants an enduring, developing relationship with us. But I think I'm restrained by the fear of pain. You know from our conversations all that I've gone through at the hands of my parents, and especially my mom.

> These are the people who supposedly love me more than anyone this side of Heaven. In my mind I can create a compelling argument that shows God loves me beyond reason. But I don't want to get hurt again — and again and again — by trusting people and being let down, and I know that fear has prevented me from experiencing the full proportions of God's love for me.

> I was reading a devotional one morning last week which was pretty lame, but it had a verse that bowled me over: Isaiah 63:9. Very unobtrusively that verse notes that God suffered and that He feels our pain. That got me to thinking about the nature of pain, and I started exploring the lives of Abraham, Isaac, Jacob, Job, Jeremiah, Paul, and of course Jesus. Each of them endured unjustifiable pain and suffering, and God felt it, too, and responded on their behalf.

> That has allowed me to jump the fence on this one, getting beyond the sense that I was in this alone. As much as I knew better, analytically, I could feel the love than overcomes the

pain. Seeing that track record of repeated experiences of the pain and the love that followed has helped me immensely.

No new information, just new interpretation, or maybe new eyes to see what I'd seen before. Anyway, the journey goes on and now I have new stumbling blocks to overcome, but that was a biggie. I don't recall you mentioning the fear of pain and suffering as an obstacle to loving God and humanity, but if you ever fall into that rut, maybe this will help you climb out quicker than I did.

AUGUST 27, 11:14 P.M.

My walk with the Lord has been much stronger since I've allowed Him to penetrate my emotional defenses and deliver not just heart-felt positive emotions toward God and others, but a yearning and a commitment to become a channel of love to them. Americans often think of love as an emotion, but it's really more than that: it is a commitment to others.

This latest episode of growth occurred once I allowed God to expand my faith even more. That expansion was facilitated by a lot of prayer and meditation, hours of dialogue with trustworthy and spiritually mature friends, continued Bible study, and other reading. Clearly, the breakthrough in aligning my heart with God's is not complete, but the progress made has been a result of integrating my mind and heart toward this goal. The bottom-line effect has been to minimize negative or inappropriate feelings such as hurt, anger, abandonment, rejection and insignificance. Love, joy and peace wedged their way into my heart, replacing the emptiness that resided there for so long.

Imagine that. My head and heart are now partners in this realignment with God. That's got to count for something.

CHAPTER 12

LIVING THE LOVE: ALIGNING MY BODY

SEPTEMBER 1, 7:50 P.M.

Personally, I've always thought that my behavior has been pretty tightly aligned with my intellectual understanding: in relation to the integration quest, I have believed that I already had half of the equation figured out!

Apparently not.

The more I have worked through how to align my behavior with God's love for me and His will for my life, the more holes I can see in my performance.

Much of the misdiagnosis stems from my having confused some behaviors for certain outcomes. In the same way that I discovered early on that there is a huge gap between change and significance, so have I misunderstood the differences between action and progress, busyness and growth, effort and impact, as well as success and obedience.

The farther I get on the transformation trail, the more I recognize that my life is further out of alignment than I ever would have imagined.

On the face of it, the whole matter of aligning my behavior with God's love is simple enough: what I do and give to God and people should reflect the nature of God's love for me and others. My actions should deliver love.

What I do for others is the fruit of the transformation that has taken place in me; the more comprehensive and tangible my expression of that love becomes, the more complete and convincing is my transformation.

Love is a concrete step, not an abstract concept. It must be active but it must also be in harmony with God's will and standards. This is apparent through many of the verses I've studied that emphasize how important our doing the right thing is to God. I've been keeping notes!

- He accepts us when we do what is right in His eyes (Genesis 4:7, Acts 10:35).

- If we listen to His instructions and principles and then do what He views as right — i.e., obey Him — then He will provide what we need (Exodus 15:22-26, Deuteronomy 6:18, Psalm 84:11).

- We can experience God's presence by doing what is right in His eyes (Psalm 15:1-2).

- We can experience joy by doing what is right in His eyes (Psalm 106:3).

- It is imperative that we speak truth, for that is right (Proverb 12:17).

- Doing right is more meaningful to God than any sacrifices we offer (Proverb 21:3).

- When we do what's right, God celebrates our choice (Proverb 23:16).

- Suffering for doing what is right is a privilege that God will not overlook (1Peter 4:19).

- We are to use our entire body to accomplish what is right for God (Romans 6:13).

- The Bible teaches us what is right and that we must do it (1 Timothy 3:16).

- Doing what is right is important for our salvation and that of others (1 Timothy 4:16).

- We have a simple choice: sin or do what's right (Jeremiah 18:11, Daniel 4:27, 1 Corinthians 15:34).

That's a lot of biblical muscle behind the idea of doing what's right in God's eyes. There is tremendous benefit; there are no discernible spiritual disadvantages.

To express my love to God through my physical capabilities, then, I can think of love in terms of what I give or do for God's benefit and then what I give or do for other people's benefit. Sometimes a single act benefits both God and others.

SEPTEMBER 19, 9:58 P.M.

Being Jennifer the Nerd (though hopefully on the road to recovery), I sat down and spent an entire Saturday working through what fits in these categories. It was an interesting exercise. After examining the entire list — which went on for pages — I synthesized them into two basic groups. Here's what I came up with.

JENNIFER'S BEHAVIORAL COMMITMENT

How I Will Love God through Physical Means

- Prove myself to be trustworthy by doing what I say I will do, and doing what I should do.

- Seek to deny sin; always strive to obey scriptural commands.

- Share the good news about Jesus's death and resurrection and grace to those who are not followers of Jesus.

- Devote myself to actively worshiping God throughout the day, every day.

- Lovingly and respectfully speak and pursue the truth and purity in all situations.

- Confess my sins to God every day to seek His forgiveness; and commit to not sinning in that manner again.

- Manage all of the resources God has entrusted to my care — time, money, relationships, ideas, information, opportunities — wisely, allocating resources strategically and generously as He provides the opportunities to do so.

- Accept times of persecution and suffering as a way of sharing in God's suffering.

- Make decisions only after waiting to hear from the Lord.

- Pray every day, throughout the day, spending most of my time listening.

- Refuse to take credit for things that the Lord has done through me.

- Read the Bible every day and commit portions of it to memory.

- Enjoy life, no matter what the circumstances are.

- Reserve the Sabbath day for time with God.

- Focus on advancing the kingdom of God, not the kingdom of Jennifer.

- Use the spiritual gifts the Lord has given me to advance His Church.

How I Will Love People through Physical Means

- Become someone other people can trust.

- Help others to avoid or deny sin and to know how to obey scriptural commands.

- Share the good news about Jesus's death and resurrection and grace with those who are not followers of Jesus.

- Become a model of spiritual commitment through worship, prayer, study, service and engagement with a spiritual community.

- Lovingly and respectfully speak and pursue the truth and purity in all situations.

- Readily forgive those who offend me: show mercy and compassion, and endure persecution and injustice with grace.

- Pursue justice without malice or arrogance.

- Bless people by sharing the resources God has entrusted to my care.

- Demonstrate moral integrity in all choices and actions.

- Be patient and kind.

- Serve others as God provides opportunity to do so, without expecting appreciation, recognition or rewards.

- Honor those who have done honorable things.

- Respect and honor my parents.

- Celebrate the victories of others, even if they spell defeat for me.

- Work for peace, restoration and reconciliation where relationships are broken.

Honestly, sharing this list with my inner circle instigated heated debate. I understand their angst, but I also recognize that no such list will ever cover the entire landscape of possibilities.

For me, at this moment in my journey, the list seems right. I have no doubt it will morph as time goes on. For the time being, if I could simply satisfy the items on this list, I'd be pretty pleased. As it stands, the list seems like the unassailable mountain, but if I simply take it one step at a time, the Lord will surely help me climb as far as I can possibly get.

WORKING OUT FAITH AND LOVE

September 23

Dear Kevin and Kathy:

I thought I'd share with you what's going on in relation to my desire to align my physical activity with my need to love God and people more completely. Do you mind taking the time to read my ramblings?

Remember I told you about the lists I put together of the ways I would try to make my physical love to God and people more specific? I'm someone who needs structure and order, so lists make sense. Lauren couldn't hack doing them. I understand that; everyone has their own way. She has been experimenting with different approaches, such as reviewing her experiences in her journal every day, and I pray that works for her.

Anyway, the lists have been helpful touch points for me. How much have they helped me change? Not as much as I'd like, but more than I would have without those commitments staring me in the face several times a day!

I have noticed that I listen more attentively to annoying people. I've become a better team player by worrying less about getting the credit for my work. I have been more courageous about speaking about my faith. And I have made fewer but better decisions by waiting until I feel an inner peace from God about my choice.

I bought one of those Bibles that walks you through the scriptures in a year (even though we're already in the second quarter) and have been diligently reading my way through the Bible, taking notes on things that strike me as being especially relevant to my journey.

Maybe the biggest change has been how I spend my Sundays. The day used to be time to catch up on what had slipped through the cracks during the week. I've now settled into a rather comfortable, and comforting routine of not doing work or getting stressed about catching up, but instead spending more time relaxing, praying, silently enjoying the life God has provided me.

The brushfire with Thom is now a thing of the past. I tried to handle it with grace and humility. That shocked some people. They're not used to such a display of kindness in the corporate jungle. At the risk of calling it prematurely, I think things have worked out great. God brought Thom to a place of embarrassment and even apology; others have scorned him, and I have been the one to defend him. Not for the outrageous lies. But I've asked people to cut him some slack and for all of us to work harder at developing a more compassionate, transparent and supportive environment. I know that a couple of the aggressive self-promoters — Ron and Carly, for instance — have taken note of the change in office politics and have been lying low of late. Maybe this will have some positive ripple effects.

In the midst of our tough economic conditions, I've also worked harder at helping those in need. Saturdays have transitioned from entertain-me-to-death days to who-can-I-serve days. I'm not exactly eliminating poverty single-handedly, but I have been able to give some assistance to a few dozen needy people by helping out at the Community Service Center (on the first Saturday of each month) and through the church's food pantry (every second and fourth Saturday).

Those are humbling times, when I see how mightily God has blessed me for no apparent reason. I rehearse the Phil Ochs song in my head, the one where he sings the classic axiom, There but for the grace of God go I. And I have increased my financial support to several organizations, even though it probably ensures that my retirement fund won't be as fat. No worries, though: God will provide what I need.

My parents are thrilled about this new era because they actually hear from me every week now. That has been a blessing to me, too, although Mom drives me crazy every once in a while when she gets on her kicks.

A few of the items on the list have been hard to operationalize — not so much in knowing what to do, but in pushing myself to do them. But that's "part of the journey," as you keep reminding me. At least there's noticeable progress.

Overall, then, I'd have to say that I'm probably moving ahead, inch by inch, toward becoming the woman God wants me to be. I know beyond a doubt that God loves me and that He constantly blesses me. I am doing all I can to share my love with Him and with others.

Working out how to feel it, know it and do it has been a challenge that I seem to master on a situation-by-situation basis! I'm not always successful, but I have consistently been attentive to the process and objectives. Hopefully practice makes perfect.

It certainly is a process!

Love, Jennifer

CHAPTER 13

EXPERIENCING THE LOVE: ALIGNING MY SPIRIT

OCTOBER 28, 5:32 A.M.

One of the most enlightening pit stops on this journey has been my examination of how my soul fits into this entire transformation process. It has been a revelation mostly because I really never knew or thought much about my soul.

From my earliest years I thought of a soul as some kind of invisible attachment that took on a life of its own — well, my life in another dimension, I guess — after my physical life was finished. I never worried about my soul because it seemed like it resided in the spiritual realm and was beyond either comprehension or influence.

As I dug deeper, though, I learned that for many years we have maligned the soul. It really stands for the totality of our life.

Our misunderstandings about the nature and significance of the soul were initially brought about by the Greeks and their interpretation of life. They were the ones who compartmentalized everything — physical life (via the body), spiritual life (represented by the soul), a thought life (through the intellect or mind), emotional life (driven by the heart), moral life (defined by adherence to external values), and so forth.

I've learned that the Bible actually has several words for soul and even uses the term "spirit" interchangeably with it in some passages. But the scriptures also make clear that when we are saved by Jesus, our entire being is saved, not just our soul.

Sometimes we speak as if our soul is saved and we have to endure the physical life until the shell (body) is removed and the soul gets on with eternity. That's not God's teaching at all.

When Jesus said that we should love God and people with all of our soul, He meant with our entire life!

But that raises another interesting consideration: once we surrender to God and submit to His Spirit, the Holy Spirit literally lives within us. (I checked; there are at least two dozen verses that confirm this!) In essence, God has taken over my life. I can resist Him, but if I am truly dependent on Him and have chosen to cooperate, then it is God who lives through me. (Which is mind-blowing, isn't it?)

So, my life is fully empowered or driven by God to the extent to which I allow Him to live through me. My life ceases to be mine in more than just concept; it becomes a true partnership in which He will assume as much control as I give Him.

So what does that mean?

NOVEMBER 10, 9:45 P.M.

What does it mean for the Holy Spirit to live in me?

Let's start out by checking the Bible. There are a couple hundred verses defining the Holy Spirit's work. The essence of His duties seems to include the following:

- Filling our mouth/mind with words to speak.

- Providing us with supernatural abilities — "spiritual gifts" — to serve the Church body.

- Giving us direction and instruction on how to behave.

- Producing feelings and attitudes such as joy, peace, humility, and hope.

- Providing continuity by never leaving us or refusing to guide us.

- Giving us boldness when we represent Christ.

- Identifying truth.

- Protecting us from harm and bad choices.

- Sculpting our thoughts so they please God and serve Him — and us — well.

- Praying on our behalf in ways beyond human capacity.

- Setting us apart from those who have rejected Christ and guaranteeing our salvation.

What do I make of this? Maybe the whole transformation challenge is easier than I've made it out to be. Yes, all dimensions of my life have to be integrated. But isn't that something the Holy Spirit will do, if I let Him? It sure seems that way.

Perhaps the biggest responsibility I must accept is to wholeheartedly recommit myself to following the Holy Spirit every day. My best hope is to not only harbor the Spirit within me, but to turn Him loose to do through me what only He can accomplish. My hope is to arrive at a single-mindedness with God.

Hebrews 12:14 says that we must "work at living a holy life, for those who are not holy will not see the Lord." Elsewhere the scriptures point out that we cannot be holy unless God fills us and His Spirit controls us. It is then that we become holy — set apart — by the presence, power and performance of His Spirit.

The verse in the book of Hebrews makes clear that if we want to see God for eternity, facilitating this kind of Spirit-driven holiness is not optional!

Bottom line?

I must work at all the things I have previously discovered about loving people by devoting my mind, heart and strength to pursuing the will of God, and doing whatever it takes to honor Him and be faithful to Him.

But I feel as if I can ease up a bit on the gas pedal knowing that I'm not pushing this car down the highway anyway. That's the Holy Spirit's job.

If I really did what I thought I did at the place on this journey where I surrendered and submitted to God so that I am wholly dependent on Him through His Holy Spirit, then a positive outcome is a lot more likely than I feared. But because my life is still lived in the context of a spiritual battle for my allegiance, making that commitment to the Spirit every day, reaffirming my desire and intention to cooperate as fully as possible, becomes a necessary and invaluable obligation.

The journey, therefore, will continue. And perhaps I can enjoy it more, now that I know it's all about God's power and performance facilitated by my active acquiescence.

SECTION 3

ROLL UP YOUR SLEEVES

CHAPTER 14

OWNING THE LAST HALF
OF THE JOURNEY

I n Section 1, we traveled through the Ten Stops necessary to overcome our resistance to giving God control on the journey to wholeness. In Section 2, we followed Jennifer as she struggled through those Stops. Now let's close this adventure together by thinking about some of the hands-on efforts that can help people grow at each stop *beyond* Stops 4 and 5.

(Remember, Stop 4 is becoming a forgiven follower of Christ through your confession of sins and invitation to Christ to be your Lord and savior, followed by Stop 5, which involves a typical engagement in church and personal growth activities.)

Our goal? To shift our full energy from previous acts of denial and resistance (which, once we extracted the hope of salvation from God, led to living an unholy and deceived life) to taking a more righteous course of action—in other words, surrendering control to God, placing Him firmly in command of your life, and appreciating every minute of that cooperative venture in experiencing the fullness of a life lived with maximum faith.

Keep in mind that transformation is a process, not a simple formula that produces the desired outcome every time. H.L. Mencken once said: "For every human problem there is a neat, simple solution, and it is always wrong." [16] Being achievement oriented, Americans are suckers for promises of a simple, guaranteed handful of steps to success, wealth, health, or happiness. Rest assured, nearly 2,000 years of human effort since Jesus died and resurrected has proven that there is no such formula. Perhaps the best we can do is understand what is meant to happen at each of the stops on the journey and commit to doing whatever we can to cooperate with God toward making consistent progress down the pathway to righteousness.

As we explore the nitty-gritty of the final five stops, let's consider the interplay between three necessary dimensions:

1. The **attitude shifts** that facilitate growth.
2. The **behavioral shifts** that advance maturity.
3. The **fruit** that typically emerges when a person embodies the objective of that stop.

STOP 6: GROWING FROM DISCONTENT
ATTITUDE SHIFTS

The good news about the agitation experienced is that it is likely prompted by the Holy Spirit. God is never satisfied when we are just putting in time and feeling comfortable, or going through the motions while taking His blessings for granted. The holiness journey is a white-knuckles adventure on earth. At the end of the ride there may be peace, serenity, love and joy, but along the way there will be tension, disappointment, conflict, uncertainty and more. All of those emotions and experiences may be put in our path to challenge us to grow. Naturally, there will be temptations and trials thrown at you by the enemy, but we ought not to give that adversary too much credit. God is in charge. He may allow various temptations to confront you, but it is always with a divine purpose in mind.

So the first perspective to embrace is the fact that your discontent with the manifestations of your faith — your church, your Bible reading, your Christian friends, your relationship with God — is not a sign of weakness. Quite the opposite: it's more likely a sign of the life that needs to burst forth within you.

Next, wrap your mind around the notion that you refuse to settle for "good enough" any longer. Simply attending church services every week is not good enough. Aimlessly reading the Bible to glean more knowledge is not good enough. Volunteering a few hours a month to work alongside your church friends to serve others out of a sense of Christian duty is not good enough. Praying to God before meals, in public gatherings, or in times of crisis or helplessness is not good enough.

God made you to be a champion and to lead the victorious life. Settling for the humdrum life of routine religion is inadequate; it insults God and it cheats you. Never again will you settle for "good enough."

Further, the appropriate mindset is that if there is a faith problem staring you in the face, the genesis of the problem is more likely to be internal than external. Look in the mirror for the culprit; don't blame God. And don't pass off the blame on others, as in "I'm not connecting with God because the sermons are lousy," or "My church never pushes me to grow beyond where I am," or "The spiritual hypocrisy of my friends is dragging me down." Whatever they are, the spiritual problems you face are most likely your own doing. Recognizing that is a necessary step to addressing the problem and committing the required resources to deal with it.

The emptiness or frustration you feel reflects your failure to partner with God to grasp the meaning, purpose, wisdom, character, and fulfillment He intends for you to have. Don't instigate a Watergate-sized cover up; acknowledge, at least between you and God, that you are sensitive to those feelings and need His help to sort them all out. Admit that you are incapable of solving these issues without Him leading the way, and that you are ready to follow His lead. Allow yourself to embrace a desperation to be all that God has in store for you.

BEHAVIORAL SHIFTS

The challenge at Stop 6 is to get beyond casual Christianity to a more sincere, deeper relationship with God that reshapes your life. There are steps you can take to move down that trail.

Read the Bible for wisdom and connection, not just information.

Most of us are raised to treat the Bible like a reference book: we consult it when we want to know something. Or we read it like a rule book, or an impersonal history lesson, or a telephone directory, memorizing the content that we believe will be useful for us in the future.

A more sophisticated approach to God's Word, though, is to see it as His personal letter to you — an intimate piece of correspondence sent from a loving father to his distant, beloved child. It is a heart-felt revelation of His own passions and dreams for you, placed in historical context, so that you may continue His legacy in ways that honor Him and advance your own best interests, which He has already prepared for you. Experience the richness of the wisdom and the depth of the love it conveys. Enjoy the bonding that it emotionally and supernaturally creates between you and your Father.

Pray for the things you need to mature in your relationship with God.

God has offered you all kinds of treasures for the journey. One of those is the opportunity to ask Him for anything that advances His will for your life and to know that He will grant that request. But what advances His will? Those things that draw you closer to Him and mold you into the person He made you to be. When you pray for the guidance, strength, wisdom, discernment and opportunities to become that person, you can be assured He is eager to comply.

Fast in order to focus.

There are many spiritual disciplines, one of which is fasting. You can fast from many things, not just food. Some people fast from movies, TV or music; others abstain from hobbies, sex, the Internet or other pleasures. The intent of this self-denial routine is to bring our minds back to God. Often, fasting is associated with repentance, but it can also be undertaken to ask God to help you change.[17] Abstaining from something you desire can become a means of remembering to focus on God's will and seeking His direction.

Listen carefully.

God never expects us to grow without His assistance. After all, when you accepted His Son as your savior, God the Holy Spirit — an advisor and counselor — came to reside within you to assist you on the journey. But you have to listen for God's voice.

In the midst of the daily cacophony of life, His words are sometimes lost in the noise. He will not shout to get your attention. Prove you care about what He thinks and trust His advice by creating enough space and silence to enable Him to speak to you clearly. He may have instigated the discontent you feel, but He does not want you to wallow or get lost in it. It has a greater purpose which He wishes to reveal to you and use for your sanctification. Have the ears to hear.

Examine yourself regarding the components that matter to God.

If the reason for your discontent is your own spiritual immobility, then you need to inventory your spiritual life. Do a thorough and honest assessment of your life goals, core values, personal relationships, spiritual objectives, and typical religious practices. Are they aligned with God's best plans for you? Do you know what those plans are? You cannot effectively change the things you do not understand. Get to know your condition as well as God does so that you can make the appropriate alterations.

Open yourself to receiving God's grace.

Americans may be the world's leaders in self-reliance. However, our abilities and smarts can take us only so far — and often those qualities lead us astray from God's best plans for our lives. To move beyond discontent, we have to be open to absorbing all the grace, mercy, forgiveness, compassion and understanding that God wants to deliver.

Sometimes we get stuck in churchiness because the routines and frantic activity mask our need for a confrontation with who we are or what we are hiding from. In those cases, it may take accessing God's grace for us to have the strength and willingness to move through our points of pain or fear. Remember that showering us with love and grace is one of His great joys. Don't deprive Him — or yourself — of that joy.

FRUIT: THE EVIDENCE OF GROWTH

Every episode of personal growth is marked by tangible results. Gleaning what God has in store for you during your period of discontent will produce such evidence.

The first indication of spiritual health is your impatience with religious games. Accepting church politics, empty routines, meaningless repetitions, and other vacuous practices does not make you a saint; it makes you a robot. The point of the Christian faith is not to be a good church member; it's to be a transformed child of God whose mission is to bless God and other people in ways that change human history. If you are irritated by requirements and expectations that become an obstacle for you to become that child of God — well, good for you. You're on your way to Stop 7.

To make continual progress, though, you would do well to incorporate a regular process of self-evaluation in your life. What really matters? How can you measure it? What are some of the clues or signs that indicate you are moving in the right — or wrong — direction? You cannot become perfect, and you will not sustain significant change overnight, but you will benefit from having a series of indicators that you regularly examine to ensure that you are headed toward transformation rather than comfort.

To see if you are ready to pursue Stop 7, explore your primary focus from hour to hour. Is it figuring out how to make the most of your life through a deeper connection with Jesus? Is it a desire to stop wasting time and energy on promoting yourself within the world system in favor of knowing God more intimately? When you have consistent evidence that your priorities have shifted such that your concern is less personal and more about your ties with God, then you can start to focus on the challenges of the next stop on the journey.

STOP 7: GROWING THROUGH BROKENNESS
ATTITUDE SHIFTS

Upon your arrival at Stop 7, your goal is to overcome your discontent by deepening your intimacy with God. Early on in your time at Stop 7 you will discover that the next challenge will be to pave the way for the maturing of that relationship by allowing God to empty you of your indulgence in sin, self, and society. That's what brokenness looks like: putting an end to those things and adopting a new passion: holy living. (Remember, holiness does not mean perfection; it means being set apart from everything else by God, for God.)

Brokenness will not occur until you make some further mental and emotional adjustments. For starters, you have to acknowledge that you cannot attain the life you want — the life He has prepared for you — without placing Him at the center of your life. He has always wanted the best for you, but you have clouded the picture through your dependence on everything but Him. He has never abandoned you, though. If you are really ready to take things to another level, He is ready to, too. But you must acknowledge with you mind, heart, body and soul that you want what He wants, and that you cannot get any farther in the journey without Him being the One who powers everything.

Part of that shift is asserting, at least to yourself and God, the spiritual poverty that has characterized your life. Admitting that you have not made much space for God and have not given Him permission to affect your life is crucial toward moving forward.

The sign of your readiness for this cleansing of your life starts with a willingness to endure the pain, suffering, sorrow, and even persecution. These are often the tools required to jettison the garbage from your life and reset your system to holiness. In the course of this process you will have experience anguish over your sin and take on a hatred of your sinful behavior. That change means losing interest in anything that gives you more joy or fulfillment than you get from your relationship with God.

The objective of brokenness is to give control of your life back to God – not out of weakness but out of trust and hope. As long as you retain control of your life, you will never know the strength and freedom that comes from utter dependence upon God. Deciding that you are committed to allowing Him to have His way with you and to remake you however He sees fit is a big-time decision. Truthfully, you cannot move forward toward wholeness until you implement that determination.

Brokenness is not a fun experience, but it is necessary to grow. Keep in mind that this is not a punishment from God; it is His gift to enable you to have the mind of Christ and the freedom and joy that comes with that. No pain, no gain.

BEHAVIORAL SHIFTS

Being transformed through the experience of brokenness comes in many ways. As mentioned earlier in this book, the research shows that a majority of Christians go through life crises — a debilitating illness, the agonizing death of a loved one, personal bankruptcy, imprisonment,

an ugly divorce, or loss of material possessions in a natural disaster —
meant to capture their attention and reorder their priorities.

Our resilience in the face of hardship, though, often prevents us
from building a better future on the foundation of such difficulties.
Most people then experience additional crises that afford the opportunity to be broken and become dependent upon God. The obvious
advice is that when you encounter abnormal circumstances, consider
whether this may be God's provision to facilitate brokenness that leads
to healing and growth. Allow Him to use those situations to shepherd
you to a better place in life.

Whether He imposes crises or not — after all, some people are
spiritually sensitive enough to understand the process and to seek brokenness without enduring such catastrophes — you have to abandon
your rights. American society is big on establishing, protecting and
utilizing the rights that come with citizenship. In the kingdom of God,
though, you voluntarily abandon all behavioral rights. God alone determines what you deserve and what you receive. Your best interests are
provided for not by some legal protections but by trusting the love of
God. Don't engage in conversations or thoughts about how unfair life
is, or the injustice of particular circumstances. Trust God with every
dimension of your life and let Him give you what is right and just in His
own way and timing.

To optimize the difficult experiences you will face, upgrade your
prayer life. Spend ample time alone with God each day, asking for insight, revelation, forgiveness, and wisdom. You may have to be creative
to get times alone with Him. Some of us have learned to use drive time
as a quiet getaway with the Lord, turning off the radio to steal a few
minutes of interactive time. Others use a portion of their lunch hour as
their private time with God. Whatever it takes, be creative and make it
happen. And be sure to use your prayer time effectively, balancing both
expressing yourself honestly as well as listening carefully.

Many of those whom I interviewed noted that journaling was a crucial aspect of their brokenness period. They relied upon their journals to capture what they believed God was revealing; how they felt about the realities God was making them confront; the hope their brokenness was bringing; the scripture passages that were meaningful on this leg of the journey; and even their observations about how other people were handling similar circumstances. The act of writing down their lessons and insights proved for many of them to be a way of cementing that progress in their mind and hear, or serving a touchstone to return to when their pain or resistance required a resource that would point them in the right direction.

Another action that proved enormously helpful for many broken Christ followers was to walk alongside of another believer who'd already endured their own primary or initial time of brokenness. (I phrase it that way because in some ways we must be broken on a regular basis; we are so conditioned by society and trained to rebuild that we have to allow God to keep bringing us back to complete dependence, even after we arrive in that place initially.) That kind of tender and wise support can give us confidence and courage to continue to give in to God while also being held accountable for the choices we make. The stories and advice provided by those mentors often protect us from needless suffering or from further prolonging this part of the journey. And when you arrive at a point of celebration, nobody can share the joy more meaningfully than those who have been through the same battle zones as you have emerged from.

FRUIT: THE EVIDENCE OF GROWTH

Among the things that happen when someone has been broken is that God initiates a healing process in his or her life. In this case, healing looks like a change in character. Often the most overt shift is from self-absorption to humility. Anyone who has been through the ravages of brokenness assumes a different self-view, with a realistic sense of self ushering in modesty and a subdued nature.

Successfully broken people never again stray far from the process of brokenness. In other words, when you find one of these people, their humility drives them to a deep and sincere repentance on a regular basis, sometimes daily. Confession of their failings before God becomes part of their everyday experience. They confess silently to God; they discuss their struggles with other believers. "Just keeping it real" means something deeper and more special to these people than is true among the millions in today's culture who utter that phrase carelessly.

Another dimension of their healing, though, is witnessed in their more relaxed disposition. That stems from being able to turn over control of all the complexities of life to God. There is not a reduction in energy or enthusiasm about life; there is simply a recognition that they don't have to worry about as many elements of life because they really cannot influence their outcome, no matter how hard they try. This is attributable to a sense of dependence on God and is one of the chief manifestations of being broken of self.

Departing from the comprehensive influence of society is frequently realized through the adoption of a new identity. It is often assumed that when a person becomes born again they take on the persona of Christ. In reality, though, few born-again individuals demonstrate such a transfer of identities until they experience brokenness. Of course, the fullness of that new identity comes from the triple bonus experienced by abandoning the grip of sin, self, and society. Because that process takes time and emptying oneself of those three influences does not happen simultaneously, the new identity as a holy person seeking to imitate Christ evolves slowly.

In my surveys, I sometimes find that this is shown by a person who formerly thought of himself first and foremost as either an American, an employee, a parent, a consumer or a good citizen to one who portrays himself as a Christian above all else.

One other piece of evidence that they have been broken is their more robust view of God. From personal experience they are likely to speak of a God who is holy and just, but also loving and gentle. They comprehend His authority in ways that most cannot; and they grasp Solomon's constant admonition to possess a fear of God — an awe and reverence for a Creator so powerful and demanding yet so loving and forgiving. When they describe the nature of God, theirs is not just a recitation of qualities memorized about God; it is a portrait of a personal God they have met in their pain and struggle, a Lord whom they have come to appreciate in ways that their Sunday school lessons never adequately conveyed. They know, based on their new experience, that the only real soul mate is Jesus Christ.

STOP 8: GROWING THROUGH SURRENDER AND SUBMISSION
ATTITUDE SHIFTS

This is a tough place to be, especially for American men. Even the terms used to describe the activity — surrendering and submitting — are harsh to the ears of independent, freedom-loving, power-seeking, self-reliant people. But after God reveals who we really are and how we have lived in such consistent disobedience and selfishness, we have only two options: make a final stand against Him, or accept His gracious offer of continued grace and support by handing over the keys to God.

After enduring the trials of brokenness, we must again undergo some critical transitions in our thinking. Surrendering control of your life and submitting to His call and His ways are the natural stepping stone after the brokenness and healing that you have recently experienced. You will ease into this transition and it will take years for you to fully inhabit it. Settle in; this stop is where you really become holy — separate from the world, set apart for God.

At this juncture we are not just surrendering to the idea of God having complete control in our life. We are literally under new ownership.

We are agreeing that from now on, we are His property from head to toe, inside and out, awake and asleep. Finally the old self is replaced by something new that we do not get to design, manipulate, administrate, or position. Past concerns like public image and popularity are of no concern to the new Owner. We no longer need to invest time, effort, money, and consideration into promoting self, satisfying the world, or hiding our sin. All we have to do is follow Jesus like a shadow.

Nearly impossible as it is, we have to grasp the ultimate truth for us at this stage: we are now fully His, truly a slave to Christ, freed from the challenges of making every decision based on our best judgment and ability. Like a franchise that is responsible for following every corporate order to the smallest detail, we are His. Signed, sealed and delivered, no exceptions, we have forfeited our worldly independence in exchange for eternal significance and dependence. This is the time to "get over yourself," once and for all.

Accept your new identity with enthusiasm; your surrender and submission to God gives you benefits that are unavailable elsewhere. Remember, the strangest condition of your surrender is that you have surrendered to a friend who loves you, not an enemy poised to exploit you or harm you. You surrendered out of a desperate personal need, not out of coercion. This is perhaps the only surrender in human history in which the people surrendering have reason to celebrate that act of subjugation. Put on your happy face; your surrender and subsequent submission to God is the next chapter of the good news story that began when you invited Jesus Christ to be your savior. Now you are truly enthroning Him as the lord of your life.

Handing over control does not mean having a lobotomy after which you mindlessly follow God. This surrender and submission procedure instills a new life in you. The essence of the agreement is that you are now committed to fully cooperating with God. It is now a genuine partnership, where God is the managing partner and you are a junior partner responsible for representing Him in the world. He will dominate you, but through love and caring. Do not expect life to be any easier — just more meaningful and with a boatload of new possibilities to express the fullness of yourself in service to the Almighty Creator.

For this to work, get used to recommitting to your status as a slave of Christ everyday — perhaps multiple times per day. Our inescapable physical context — the world — will not stop trying to win us back. The battle for your heart, mind and soul will continue; God's eternal enemy has no intention of letting you get away so easily. So, to help this transformation stick, set your mind on your new identity and affirm it continually.

Take comfort in the fact that now that you are under new ownership, that Owner is responsible for the ultimate results. If you are faithful — obedient, loving, devoted to serving, worshipful, trusting Him — then He must orchestrate the outcomes. How much pressure and anxiety does that relieve?

At the same time, this means that you can follow Jesus's prescription to take life one day at a time. Don't worry about the future; the new Boss owns and controls that as well, regardless of your expectations and fears. It will all turn out according to plan — His plan.

Like they say, don't sweat the small stuff. When you are surrendered and submitted to God, it's all small stuff.

BEHAVIORAL SHIFTS

This is such a radical switch: what can you do to facilitate the full and proper transfer of control, producing the benefits that coincide with the transition? Try some of these routines that surrendered believers indicated were important in their renaissance.

First, if you have surrendered to God, then several behaviors will compete for the title of *Most Important Thing to Do Today*. The finalists in that competition are worshiping God, obeying His will and principles, loving God and people, and joyfully serving the Lord. None is more important than the other. None is complete without the others, or gives God greater pleasure or glory than the others. For those of us who sometimes recall things better through the use of acrostics, try this: live a SLOW life (as in Serve, Love, Obey, and Worship). Nothing would better facilitate cooperation and partnership with God than a SLOW life. Granted, for some of us, this is a new set of habits to develop, but there will never be a more important series of habits to embrace.

Perhaps the least common of those four components is leading a life that incorporates continual worship. How can you practically worship God throughout the day? Beyond the old standards of expressing gratitude for His blessings and greatness, being obedient, reading the scriptures, and offering prayers of thanks — all of which are valuable endeavors that honor Him — here are some less-common practices relied on by people who are a bit farther along the journey than you may be at this point.

- *Reflect on your blessings.* Jesus was born, suffered, died, and resurrected for you. You have been given the assurance of a remarkable life with God after your time on earth expires. You are able to know, serve, and be loved by a God who defines justice and grace. Every day you decide what to devote your thoughts to. You can worship God by making Him the center of your thought life. When you meditate on God, be sure to revel in respect, awe, fear and love for Him.

- *Repent. You are forgiven.* You are accepted. And you are still a sinner who disobeys God. Identify those failings and repent of them — daily, hourly, or however often is appropriate. Surrender the weak aspects of your living and character. This is your way of reasserting that you have embraced His ideals.

- *Celebrate creation.* Don't get so busy or distracted with the demands of the world that you lose sight of the incredible universe God has created for us. Not only are its intricate workings beyond comprehension, but the sheer creativity and beauty of the natural world is breathtaking to behold. Surely the One who made it for our pleasure deserves a regular dose of appreciation as well as the satisfaction of watching us examine and revel in His handiwork.

- *Be humble.* God will play His part in humbling you, but the more you are able to grasp your true standing in the world in comparison to God's greatness, the more realistic you will be and the more likely you are to adopt your role of treasured servant.

- *Memorize scriptures.* This is not for the benefit of showing off in conversations or performing a parlor trick. Filling your mind with truth provides you with the ability to know how to respond to every life situation. But intentionally imprinting His Word on your mind and heart also communicates the value you place on His truths — and upon the One who declared them.

- *Make a joyful noise.* Perhaps you are, like me, congenitally incapable of singing in tune. But you can use music as a vehicle to express your heart to God nevertheless. Listen to and agree with songs that praise Him. Enjoy songs that are "secular" — and credit the creative talent and technical proficiency of the artists to God. Treat worship lyrics like poetry and simply recite it. Whatever works, recognize and utilize music for the worship tool that it is.

- *Evangelize.* When you spread the good news, you affirm the majesty and love of God through your testimony to His grace. Sharing truths about His love and forgiveness with those who do not know Him trumpets His name and nature to a hurting and spiritually estranged population.

- *Be generous.* You may not have the wealth of Bill Gates. You probably cannot allocate the time in your day however you wish. But you have plenty of resources — time, skills, material goods, relationships, information, money — that can be invested in the lives of others to improve their lot. All of those resources belong to God, of course, and He has simply asked you to manage them for Him. The generosity with which you do so becomes a reliable indicator of where your treasure is located.

In addition to continual worship, be wholly connected to God. This goes beyond frequent prayer, although that's certainly part of it. This is about having "the mind of Christ."

It's almost like booting up your computer and being connected to the Internet: you want a solid, lasting connection that enables you to navigate through life without the connection crashing. With that unbroken connection you are able to listen for His voice. God is quite a talker when you know His voice and are willing to follow His guidance.

Hearing God's voice not only requires the ability to be quiet so that you can recognize it amidst the noise of the world. It also demands that you be more God-conscious — that is, aware of His presence and in tune with His objectives for you. Of course, communication is two-way, so this integration gives you the chance to consult Him on everything. He doesn't get tired of engaging with you. Nothing is too trivial for Him. Let this connection bring you godly wisdom and a Spirit-led obedience. The connection also allows you to experience and recite His attributes as a way of praising Him and reminding yourself of the privilege you have of interacting with the Holy One.

Finally, evaluate the demands on your life and eliminate those that are not necessary to carry out God's will. Remember, as a person who has surrendered, your choices are no longer yours; as one who is submitted, your objective is now to satisfy the desires of your Master. When you obsess on that agenda you will be surprised to discover how many worthless activities that typically consumed your time and energy are cast aside.

Once you begin to jettison the extraneous, you can SLOW down; your life will be less frenetic and cluttered, more focused and reasonable, more purposeful, and more fulfilling. Easing the pace, in turn, allows you to wait on God. That facilitates finding a godly rhythm to life, rather than the frantic rhythm we try to dance to; enjoy a simpler life; and have an easier time making appropriate decisions.

FRUIT: THE EVIDENCE OF GROWTH

As a seasoned traveler on the journey to wholeness, at this point your daily schedule and observable activities will look very strange to the rest of the world. Your leisure time will be less characterized by mass media consumption and more frequently consumed by prayer, scripture, and simple pleasures, like noticing and appreciating elements of God's creation. Your mind will be less devoted to the world and more attuned to the Holy Spirit, both available to serve and aware of His presence. Consequently you will reflect greater self-control, a more genuine humility, and more profound courage and confidence, which will sometimes be expressed by taking risks that make little sense to the world but are simply matters of obedience for you.

A surrendered and submitted person of God is committed to new life goals — His goals. Those goals exist in your heart because you are readily available to Him. Those goals are carried out with joy and diligence which are evidenced in the lightness of your heart, the reduction of stress on your face, the pleasure you radiate at living purposefully, and the integrity you incorporate in every undertaking. Your spiritual gifts are consistently applied to those goals, and your gifts seem to become more prolific and impactful as time goes forth. Whatever resources you possess you wisely but generously invest in people or projects that advance a kingdom agenda. You have no anxiety about the required risks or the likely outcomes; you are secure enough in your relationship with God to believe that He loves you sufficiently to take care of you and to therefore leave the results to Him.

One of the most startling transformations evident to observers is your contentment with life. You are no longer a contestant in the rat race, always trying to get an advantage or carve your own niche in the world. Your niche has been carved for you in Heaven, and you are released from worry and anxiety on earth. This is not the same as giving up or believing in fatalism; you simply know beyond a doubt that your life is now controlled by God and you trust Him enough to believe He knows what He is doing and will take care of things if you obey His will. You are content. Temptations seem fewer in number and less appealing.

All of these indications of your transformation reflect one glorious reality: you are free. You have raced past mere happiness to utter joy and fulfillment. It is this exhilaration and lightness that allow you to move to the next stops on the journey.

STOP 9: PROFOUNDLY LOVING GOD
ATTITUDE SHIFTS

Once you reach that wonderful place where you are over self, sin, and society, you're left with a big vacuum in your life. What would you fill it with? That's what Stops 9 and 10 on the journey provide.

Having realized how unfulfilling your life was, despite your best efforts and consistent participation in church activities, you experienced the separation of your life from the unholy trinity (self, sin, society) that previously owned you. That brokenness then ushered in your decision to surrender to God and submit to His will. That, in turn, produces the greatest benefit imaginable: a profound and intimate love experience with God that endures for as long as you allow it to do so.

In the movies, a big wow moment for teenage films is finding out that the Prom King likes you. "Me? Goofy, inexperienced, immature me? The boy of my dreams, falling for me, a simple girl with pimples waiting to erupt at any moment? What an indescribable gift from God." That's Hollywood. On your journey to holiness, the love exchange that happens between you and God puts all of those other cultural infatuations to shame. It is genuine love: trusting, caring, selfless, mutual, consistent, unconditional, inexhaustible. Life just doesn't get any better than arriving at this place.

But, of course, this doesn't happen without your commitment to being in this kind of a relationship with God, and that commitment doesn't occur without a major mindshift. Building upon the experiences you had in the prior pair of stops, let me pass along the observation of how this bond takes root.

Every love connection begins with the passionate desire to develop the relationship to its ultimate end. The marriage works because the parties will accept nothing less. The relationship transcends feelings. It gets cemented by a four-fold promise: mental determination, emotional passion, physical devotion, and spiritual unity. The concentration of these components results in an insoluble bond. It is a covenant agreement of the highest order. You have chosen; nothing will stand in your way of optimizing this relationship.

To experience that type of love, recognize that your life is now one with God. What He wants becomes your highest desire. What He enjoys fills you with pleasure. What He asks of you becomes your most pressing commitment. What He gives you becomes a treasured gift. Just as He has been fully focused on enabling you to love Him, you now have the opportunity of a lifetime to reflect that same degree of obsession toward Him.

In the core of your being, then, the central idea is that every moment of every day is all about being with, understanding, enjoying, and pleasing Him. You no longer need a crisis to get your mind to lock into a God frame of thought. Your mind and heart now seamlessly lock onto His purposes and means. You are "so over" yourself and entirely focused on Him. Or, in the language of our culture, you lose yourself in Him.

If this seems like over-the-top rhetoric, it is probably because you have not yet arrived at Stop 9. Much like Jesus blowing our minds by describing the paradoxes of the godly life — the humble will rule, love your enemies, be happy when you are persecuted for Christ — our understanding of God-love is minuscule in the beginning of our journey with Him, and only grows to significant proportions and depth after we have gone the full length of the pilgrimage with Him. In other words, you cannot skip the earlier stops on the journey and rush to the final destination points; that would be a sad, one-dimensional relationship. The journey itself is what enables you to enjoy the richness of the relationship that He wants with you. It is revealed progressively.

BEHAVIORAL SHIFTS

What emerged as tentative acts of faith at Stop 8 now become full-blown ways of life at Stop 9. You exhibit complete trust in God's ways. You not only understand His will; now you take great joy in being able to commit yourself to it. You hear voices in your head, but you're not schizophrenic: it is the Lord filling your mind with His thoughts and your own soul responding with scriptures, praises, affirmations, and prayers.

You retain an earnest and eager desire to read from His word every day, knowing that He has something important and revealing to tell you. As you read those words you feel as if you have become part of the narrative, no longer an outsider looking in but now a full-fledged participant in the unfolding divine drama. Because of this new level of comprehension and acceptance you appreciate so much more about life and appreciate those things more fully.

One of your most significant behavioral transitions is the amount of time that is now devoted to God. He is your life. You no longer give him a devotional time in the morning, a few prayers during the day, and an end-of-day prayer and reflection. Your life is now inseparable from your faith and partnership with God. All time is God time.

Yes, you still focus on the details and activities related to your occupation. But now you do it in tandem with God, and with a different understanding of why it matters. Certainly you invest time and energy into your family, but it now happens with Him as your partner and His perspective on family life driving your choices. Your wristwatch still helps you remain on schedule for your earthly commitments, but your internal clock is now set to God's time.

FRUIT: THE EVIDENCE OF GROWTH

The big outcome at this place, of course, is the enormity of your relationship with Him. You have never previously experienced anything like it. And there is nothing else that can compete with it. This is the apex of your life, the mountaintop experience.

There are, however, numerous manifestations of this experience. Here are a few to look forward to.

- *Complete peace with God.* When you have both the assurance and the experience of God's full love, what's left to worry about? He offers divine guidance, supernatural wisdom, Spirit-driven discernment, absolution from sin, and a new perspective on the meaning and execution of life. We may have complete confidence in Him because we know He will supply whatever we truly need. We can grow into a calmness and serenity about life that immersion in the rat race precludes. As John Wesley commented, we are able to know a "tranquility of spirit" that evades those who do not have such a relationship.

- *Nonstop conversation.* We cannot overwhelm God with our thoughts and words; He designed us for relationship and dialogue is a necessary part of that association. When your first inclination is to go to God rather than worldly sources, you're probably enjoying this level of friendship.

- *Absence of fear.* If you are the beloved of God and have an intimate relationship with Him, what is there to fear? Death? He overcame it for you. Sin? He forgave it if you asked Him to. Material provision? He promises to take care of your real needs. Abandonment? He has pursued and longed for you since you were just an idea in His heart; He literally created you for this closeness. His love replaces the fear you had. You may retain one morsel of fear — fear born out of reverence and awe for Him — but the terror of making mistakes, bad choices, and other wrong turns in life can be locked away in a vault of past foolishness. You are now in the fear-free zone.

- *Sense of being home.* When you are with family and friends who accept you for who you are and will do their best to bless you, you are home. What could be more like home than being in the presence and heart of God, without fears and anxieties?

- *Near-effortless pursuit of His will.* Because the love relationship has become so fully reciprocal, doing the will of God becomes the most desirable objective in your life. You won't always hit a home run in this pursuit; occasionally you will strike out. But the intention and desire are unmistakable: doing whatever most pleases your Father in Heaven is job one.

- *Constant joy — and heartbreak.* What could be better than experiencing and expressing love with God? The knowledge of that unity with Christ cannot help but bring joy to your being. At the same time, you experience the heartbreak of knowing that most people are not reveling in this free gift from the Lord, despite His desperate desire for them to do so. How crushing is that? Your life, then, is lived with the paradox of the joy of love fulfilled and the pain of love unclaimed.

- *Eagerness to share His love.* Always mindful that this freedom and unity with Christ was a free gift, not something you earned or deserve, you naturally want to lead others to the same stops on the journey you have traversed. There are no shortcuts, of course, but you yearn for a greater number of your family, friends and even complete strangers to see the possibilities and commit the totality of their existence to the SLOW life. Consequently, your conversations address this potential. Your actions build opportunities for people to experience what you have been given. Part of your joy each day comes from seeing others move closer toward Him — not because it makes you successful or it increases the numbers at church, but because it helps them to fulfill their greatest possibilities in life.

STOP 10: LOVING PEOPLE AS GOD DOES
ATTITUDE SHIFTS

One of the hardest points of the journey — and probably the reason it is the final stop — is that of loving people as much as you love God or yourself, and more than you love any other aspects of life. Based on my interviews with the people who have reached this place, I think it is usually last on the map for the simple reason that people are not loveable. Only God could truly see past all the garbage and obstacles to embrace them unconditionally.

Stop 10 — extreme love of people — is possible only if you become a vessel for God's love. In other words, it is not even you who loves them as much as it is God, who now controls your life and determines your demeanor and behavior. It is He who is loving them through you, in spite of you.

When you are fully dependent upon Him, He provides you with

new eyes to see the world, new ears to hear His voice, a new mind to interpret reality, and a new heart to feel his love and pain. Outfitted with those new components, you are able to be utilized by God for things you could never hope to recognize or appropriately respond to on your own. By giving Him total control of your life, you become the mechanism He works through to display His love to others. You are simply the means, even though you will often — and undeservedly — get the credit.

But there is another attitude shift that enters the picture at this point in the journey: excitement. When you realize that you can be the one whom God uses to be an instrument of transformation, that you are the person He chooses to bless someone unexpectedly, that you are the partner whose input could be the turning point in another person's journal to holiness — for a Stop 10 person, that's worth getting out of bed for each morning.

BEHAVIORAL SHIFTS

Perhaps you have heard of the "One Anothers" — the series of statements in the New Testament that describe how we are called to treat one another. I think there is no better way to summarize what happens at this stage of the journey than to recap these scriptural commands.

It turns out that there are about twenty-five of these commands which I believe can then be categorized into four behavioral themes. [18]

- *Love and appreciate each other.* This includes the injunctions to love each other; live in harmony; accept each other; eliminate jealousy or envy; care for each other; show patience and kindness toward one another; and enjoy fellowship together. [19]

- *Protect each other.* We are to look out for each other's best interests, which includes warning each other — especially about sin, deception, and becoming hardened against God. [20]

- *Support each other in growth.* The Bible exhorts us to build up each other; offer encouragement; give help or assistance through our spiritual gifts; teach and counsel each other; do good to others; facilitate the spiritual receptivity of others; pray for and serve each other. [21]

- *Trust and respect one another.* This is accomplished by honoring each other; refusing to condemn others; being sensitive to each other's needs; seeking common ground with each other so there is no needless quarreling; speaking truth; forgiving each other; and sympathizing with each other. [22]

The toughest part is figuring out how to treat each other in these ways. The anecdotes from transformed individuals suggest that we might start by evaluating how we are spending or sharing our time and talents; how often we invite others into our life; how we perceive these people (e.g., competitors, sinners, poseurs, threats, inferior, etc.); and how we speak to them.

We can also engage in very simple resource assessment efforts, such as examining what share of our prayers are devoted to the needs and best interests of others, rather than ourselves. Further, consider how earnestly and passionately you interceded on behalf of others.

FRUIT: THE EVIDENCE OF GROWTH

People who persevere to reach this final stop on the journey are neither perfect nor done. As long as we live on earth, we will have moments of weakness or failing as well as opportunities for further growth. As much as we are able to imitate the life of Christ, we will never be the perfect replica of Jesus.

Having said that, the beauty of reaching the final stop on the pathway to holiness is that we become much closer than ever to being Christ-like. You will lead a life that provides joy and fulfillment because it is based on love, worship, service and obedience. You will be a treasured and invaluable part of a community of believers who you may lead by example as well as words. You will more often than not be the embodiment of the fruit of the Spirit, as outlined in Galatians 5, displaying those attributes through the kind of character that honors God and advances His kingdom.

For you, being a man or woman of God will no longer be an empty concept or unattainable theological objective. You can say with humility that God is still at work perfecting your faith, but that you are gratified that He has made progress with the hard clay He had to mold.

CHAPTER 15

CONSIDERATIONS FOR
CHURCH LEADERS

I f you are a church leader or have influence within a church body,
what can you do about the fact that most Christian churches in
the United States wholeheartedly believe in full-life transformation and even believe they are in the business of facilitating it — but are
not effectively enabling such growth? The solution clearly is not changing intentions. It is more complex than that.

Many Christian thinkers and church leaders would concur that
the organized church has six primary functions: 1) *worship*: facilitating genuine adoration of God; 2) *evangelism*: equipping believers to
share the gospel; 3) *discipleship*: developing and training people in the
substance and practices of the Christian faith; 4) *service*: stimulating
Christians to serve people in the both the faith community and the
world; 5) *stewardship*: investing and managing the church's resources
efficiently; and 6) *community*: providing a loving and supportive community among believers.

As we reconceptualize the local church in its conventional form to
foster individual transformation, what can communities of faith do to
advance the kingdom of God more effectively?

TRANSFORMATION AND WORSHIP

Let's start by looking at worship. We have already provided a mini-apologetic for the significance of loving God through not just acts of worship but through a lifestyle that incorporates worship. A significant person-to-person relationship is severely limited if the parties only engage with each other once a week — and especially if only in a group context. In the same way, our relationship with God cannot flourish when we limit our worship to a routine time and place, in the midst of a program designed to provide a one-size-fits-all "heartfelt commitment." The Pharisees and Sadducees were castigated by God for their legalistic adherence to rules and routines. Sadly, several national studies I have conducted decisively indicate that "worship services" are usually ineffective at facilitating a genuine connection between the worshiper and God. Further, our studies indicate that the weekend worship service is typically the only time a self-described Christian attempts to worship God.

To upgrade this situation our leaders and teachers must deploy a full-court press toward altering people's perceptions about, preparation for, and participation in worship. Honest engagement in worship is one of the best signs of our submission and surrender. Conversely, the failure to have surrendered and submitted may be one of the major blockages to authentic worship.

The research gives some guidance as how to proceed, noting that most "Christians" do not know why they should worship God, or what He considers to be valid or satisfying worship. In thirty years of working with churches around the nation I also discovered that churches do surprisingly little to determine the nature of people's experiences in the weekly worship service. Better evaluation of the value of those events and making appropriate changes would undoubtedly help the body of Christ connect more deeply and consistently with the living God.

In the last chapter we discussed some of the worshipful behaviors people at Stop 8 rely on. Churches can assist in that process by consistently motivating churchgoers to think of worship as a state of being rather than an event to attend. Many of the adults interviewed who are working their way through the advanced stops on the journey perceive worship to be a running conversation with God — a kind of extended prayer session — in which they express their love, admiration, gratitude, awe, commitment, and pleasure to Him while listening carefully for His response. While that is far from the totality of their experience, even that simple tweak would represent a major step forward for most Christians, and an important change that churches could help facilitate.

Clearly there is value to having a group experience with God. Scripture calls for believers to get together regularly, and one of the primary purposes for those gatherings is to express their love and praise to their Lord. The methods used to accomplish that goal are less important than the underlying motivation and the act of gathering to bless God. Church leaders have an obligation to liberate and assist Christ followers to engage in multiple new forms of private and public worship. There is no biblical mandate that every worship gathering include singing, preaching and fundraising; we have been granted more leeway for creativity than we have used.

In fact, there may be more ways to use technology to facilitate worship than have yet been embraced by churches. While we use a lot of technology in worship services now — ranging from sophisticated audio systems to huge video screens, from electronic instruments to podcasting sermons — it seems as if we are only beginning to harness such tools for expressing our love to God. If the objective is to call people to worship in their own time and way, how are we using Twitter, real-time online worship adventures, YouTube, or smart phone location apps (like Foursquare, BrightKite, Loopt, and Google Latitude) as catalysts for gathering or worshiping? One could argue that exploiting every new technological tool to give people another avenue through which they could worship God would justify the existence of those technologies.

TRANSFORMATION AND EVANGELISM

The research highlights the sad reality that relatively few Americans experience an episode of brokenness that positively affects their relationship with God. Doesn't that raise some fundamental and serious questions about how many genuine followers of Christ there are in America? After all, merely believing that Jesus is God, and that He lived on earth and exists today is not enough; the Bible tells us that even Satan believes those things. Saying you've made a commitment to Christ and living in ways that demonstrate that commitment are two different realities. Claiming to be saved because of having said a prayer asking for forgiveness while continuing to live without a dramatic change of heart is not the same as seeking forgiveness and turning that forgiven heart over to the one who extended the forgiveness.

American Christians verbally dismiss the possibility that they are trading in cheap grace — taking the free gift of salvation without simultaneously committing to allowing the Holy Spirit to rule their life. That is spiritual mutiny: hijacking the treasure and jettisoning the Captain. Yet the research consistently reveals that we have sustained that mutiny for well over a quarter century.

The disconnect occurs between what we say we believe and how we choose to apply those beliefs. Amazingly, little is done in our churches to correct this tacit rejection of Christ. We continue to market cheap grace, count bodies, and move ahead as if the system works. It's time to acknowledge that the institutional, programmatic approach to facilitating true faith is as broken as it can get — much more broken than the people being numbered among God's chosen ones.

For years I have been telling church leaders that evangelism without discipleship is spiritual abuse. Now we must add another caution to the list: evangelism that is not founded on a repentant sinner experiencing genuine brokenness is spiritual deception.

Does that seem harsh? It's the only way I can explain the statistics regarding the lack of distinction in lifestyle between those who claim they have confessed their sins and accepted Jesus as their savior and those who have not. Sometimes it seems as if our objective is to get non-Christians to accept Jesus Christ as their savior, but not their Lord. The inevitable result of our emphasis upon salvation without surrender is that these newcomers invite Christ into their heart, let Him in, lock Him in the guest room, and then all but abandon Him. It is not until they are freed from the bondage of self, sin, and society that they release Him from the bondage they have placed Him in, and allow *Him* to have free reign of the domain.

Throughout His earthly ministry Jesus talked about the necessity of bearing fruit as the mark of salvation, discipleship, and the love of God and people — that is, of transformation. That is where the rubber meets the road. Where is the fruit?

The objective is not to judge of people or to insinuate that we can flawlessly gauge a person's standing with God. God — and God alone — is qualified to judge the hearts and souls of human beings. But if we are to be the authentic Church, then we must support each other in our journey to wholeness. That means being discerning without being judgmental.

An important aspect of this struggle is that Americans don't take sin seriously these days. Many don't even know what it is. It is difficult to find people who are sensitive to the idea of sin, much less the practices that constitute offenses against God. And without that foundation in place, springing the news on people that they are destined for eternal condemnation and suffering because of their sinful habits comes out of left field. The related idea of experiencing personal devastation because of that sinfulness is patently ludicrous in a culture whose heart cry is to look out for the self, based upon *self*-expression, *self*-definition, *self*-help, *self*-promotion, *self*-fulfillment, and *self*-satisfaction.

So what does transformational evangelism look like? We might begin by rethinking the purpose of evangelism. During His earthly ministry Jesus did *not* emphasize judgment and condemnation; He wasn't silent on that subject but His desire was that people choose to turn to God out of love and appreciation, not dread and fear. His goal was not to force people to perceive a life with God as the lesser of two unappealing choices. That's because biblically sound evangelism is not primarily about keeping us out of hell; it is first and foremost about appropriately responding to the death and resurrection of Jesus Christ and the offer of an eternal and transformative relationship with God.

A life of devout allegiance to and cooperation with God provides countless benefits; eternal salvation is just one of them. The promise of salvation, though, ought not to be the motivation for connecting and cooperating with God. Understanding the realities and the gravity of our situation may well instill a fear of God and His condemnation, but evangelism should promote gratitude, excitement, relief, and joy over the incredible opportunity to intimately know a loving and life-sparing God who waits for us to decide that we really want the relationship He has facilitated.

What would effective evangelism look like in this age if we embrace such a mindset? Here are some thoughts for your consideration.

Many believers who engage in evangelism — and the research emphasizes that there are not many of them, relatively speaking — typically push the "free gift" component of the message. For the sake of the recipients of that message, we need to present a more balanced story, one that includes a significant discussion of brokenness, surrender, and submission. It is borderline bait-and-switch if we lure people in with the promise of grace, love, forgiveness, and redemption, then jump to an emphasis upon obedience, brokenness, submission, surrender, and service. A crucial element to include within that story is the new nature that a true believer takes on. Concepts such as dying to self, being freed from this world to become a slave of Christ, seeking to live a holy life, bearing fruit for the kingdom of God, and personally decreasing so that Christ might increase are biblical teachings that get the short shrift in American churches.

Effective outreach, though, is about much more than people hearing evangelistic sermons in churches or messages at outreach events. My research consistently finds that lifestyle evangelism — i.e., a follower of Christ living an integrated life that so attracts nonbelievers that the Christian has an opportunity to credibly discuss faith in Jesus and the contours of a transformed life — is the most effective approach available.

Lifestyle evangelism is often derided by critics as Evangelism Lite — and the data show that sometimes that criticism is justified. But when a Christ follower is leading a transformed life, she is not only displaying the heart of Christ but also interacting with others in viable and appealing ways that communicate the truths and principles of the authentic Christian life. The objective ought not to be the elimination of lifestyle evangelism, but the development of more Christians whose lifestyle is a continual statement of faith.

Meaningful evangelism these days must also dispel the false distinction between evangelism and discipleship. Unless we, as people saved by grace and openly sharing the gospel with others, are willing to walk alongside those with whom we share that good news, we are shirking our responsibility to God and the individual. The Church is composed of people who have a diversity of gifts, but we are all sufficiently experienced and gifted to journey in the company of those who are still seeking Truth. Our refusal to befriend people in that way is spiritual abandonment. Their failure to grasp the gospel and mature in a meaningful relationship with Christ could be directly attributable to our intransigence. I can imagine the Lord asking what was so important in our own journey that we left another beggar on the side of the road and continued on our way without helping the other person. I cannot imagine a reasonable excuse.

Finally, if churches are going to be effective facilitators of evangelism, they must redefine their success metrics. Simply counting the number of "decisions" or baptisms is misleading. Introducing ways of evaluating how many people are seriously engaged in an ever-deepening relationship with Christ and allowing the Holy Spirit to direct and transform their lives would provide more meaningful measures of outreach efforts.

In this regard, it behooves us to reconsider our notion of how time elapses in the evangelistic process. Is it possible that we have become so enamored of moving quickly — that is, getting one person saved and then moving on to the next unsaved person because "the time is short" — that we do a disservice to everyone involved?

Was Jesus' resurrection about immediacy? Do we believe that God controls time and will end it when He sees fit, not a moment before? Is it scripturally defensible to suggest that God will bring about the end times prematurely — which would include stopping life as we know it before people have had the appropriate opportunity to respond to His grace?

Stated differently, maybe we have to accept the fact that although we like to move fast and count success as soon as possible, transformation is a lifelong process — and progress on the journey takes longer if we begin with a weak foundation. Establishing a person as knowledgeable regarding the meaning and implications of sin, as well as the fullness of forgiveness and spiritual growth, takes time. In a world of distractions and doubt, we would be foolish to rush somebody into a relationship they do not understand or are not ready to commit to. That's not an excuse for us to be lazy or complacent regarding outreach, just a call for reasonable expectations and process.

TRANSFORMATION AND DISCIPLESHIP

In practical terms, discipleship is often translated to mean teaching people information about God. In other words, our discipleship efforts emphasize the transfer of religious knowledge. One is said to be a disciple if one is a church regular, owns a Bible, acknowledges having accepted Christ as her savior, and generally talks the talk.

One of the most important lessons I've learned after thirty years of studying both religious and secular organizations is that you get what you measure. Consider our currently popular "discipleship" metrics: worship service and class attendance, small group involvement, tithing, reading the Bible, praying regularly, knowing core biblical content, and engaging in some form of service. Those can be helpful activities, if they serve a purpose beyond being religious and providing an external image of spiritual intensity.

Don't you think the Church would be radically different — and more world-changing — if we measured brokenness, surrender, submission, God-love, other-love, dependence on God, intimate prayer, waiting on God, lifestyle worship, Spirit-reformed character, intentional silence, producing spiritual fruit, and the like?

Transferring information from one person to another does not necessarily facilitate transformation. Neither does hiring religious professionals to carry the load. The research indicates only the weakest of statistical correlations between the size of a church's staff and the spiritual growth of the congregation's members. There also is no significant connection between the popularity of church programs and individual spiritual development. Consistent attendance at church events, ranging from worship services to Christian education classes and small group meetings, doesn't show much positive influence, either. When it's all said and done, maybe we need to be reminded that programs don't change people, God does.

As we ponder a more transformative way of growing disciples, it is imperative also to address developmental realities. I have written extensively in other books about the necessity of influencing the lives of people before they reach the age of thirteen. The moral, spiritual, relational, attitudinal, and intellectual foundations for the rest of a person's life are established before a person reaches the teen age. After that point those foundations change very little. If we are serious about transformation, we should invest heavily in helping children to progress on the journey. If they do not, the chances of them ever getting far on that path are slim. Within the organized church, as well as the family unit, the most influential and significant ministry is that which takes place among children.

There are, of course, other steps we can take to improve the probability of people cooperating with God and becoming significantly transformed. Here are some.

- Training and providing personal spiritual directors or coaches for congregants.

- Structuring discipleship activities such that the family is the basic unit through which discipling happens.

- Eliminating the emphasis upon the sermon as the primary vehicle for discipleship.

- Assisting people in connecting with God through a dynamic, more frequent, less self-absorbed prayer life.

- Shifting the perceived purposes of church involvement from institutional support and program completion to connecting with God through brokenness, surrender and submission.

These steps would help redefine "church" as we know it. We need to connect believers on the pilgrimage to develop a true spiritual community rather than bland realities such as membership or comfortable friendship. The Church needs to redefine discipling to mean helping

followers of Christ to deeply and consistently love God and people
with all of their heart, mind, body and soul.

TRANSFORMATION AND STEWARDSHIP

Transformed individuals see stewardship as a simple and central matter.
It is simple in that they realize Christ followers are merely managers of
whatever resources God chooses to entrust to us for the advancement
of His kingdom. It is central in the sense that how generously we share
those resources on God's behalf reflects where our heart truly lies. In
addition, the holistic perspective embraced by believers seeking to love
God and people recognizes that stewardship is about more than just
money: it includes the management of resources such as time, relationships, skills, material goods, ideas, and information.

Churches seeking to support a person's journey to wholeness
should consider what transformation looks like in the most practical
terms, and encourage believers to invest their resources in people and
processes that efficiently produce those outcomes. In all likelihood,
that will result in resources being delivered directly to people rather
than donated for programs, buildings, and institutional operations. Just
as the early church experienced lives being fully transformed without
reliance on buildings, paid clergy, multimedia events, formal ministry
programs, or even Bibles to purchase and distribute, a transformed
person's focus on the relationship between God and people will gener-
ate a different allocation of resources than is the norm in today's con-
gregations. If our faith communities seek to embody transformation,
very different stewardship processes and results will emerge.

As challenging as it may be, then, church leaders must encourage
people on the journey to obey the guidance of the Holy Spirit and share
their resources as God directs. That may be to the conventional church,
or it may be directly to other ministry and life ventures in which they
are engaged. Highlighting the importance of giving it all away, in one

form or another, is an all-too-infrequently heard message — especially if the recipient is not automatically the local church.

TRANSFORMATION AND SERVICE

While American churches receive hundreds of thousands of volunteer hours each year, and a small but significant share of that time and energy is expended on serving the needs of people outside the congregation, our studies have shown that most Christians do not serve anyone in the community during a typical year, and it is a minority of church-goers who serve more than a handful of hours within their church during the year. Most church-going Americans believe that such acts of service are good, worthwhile and necessary, yet relatively few engage in them. Why?

First, we often struggle with inappropriate motivations. Many believers engage in acts of service out of a sense of Christian obligation; a need to belong; the desire to burnish their public image; or guilt-based pressure from church officials. Surprisingly, it is the exception to the rule to find servants whose motive is love-driven obedience to God, a passion to honor God through their service, or a simple love for people.

The needs in America, much less around the world, are huge. Can you imagine the impact of having followers of Christ willingly engage in regular and frequent opportunities to help other people, without any likelihood of personal reward or recognition? Could we instigate such service if we diminished our marketing of church programs in favor of stimulating simple love through acts of sacrificial service? How would families be impacted if the local church were committed to providing opportunities for families to serve together?

In this vein, consider that my research shows most "born-again Christians" are unaware of their spiritual gifts. If they could identify and hone those gifts and use them in service, what might happen to both the people being served and to the believer who is using the supernatural tools God granted them? What effect would waves of Christians banding together to serve the needy have not only on the needy but on society's impression of the Church and the power of the Christian faith? How much more unified would the Church become if believers were as committed to sacrificially loving people through service as they are to watching television each day? What impact would the Church have if service efforts crossed congregational and denominational lines and enabled the aggregate Church to behave as a true community of faith?

TRANSFORMATION AND COMMUNITY

Churches believe that establishing relationships among congregants is important. To facilitate those ties, various efforts are made, the most important of which (in the eyes of church leaders) are small groups so that believers can help each other through "life-on-life" experiences.

Barna Group studies indicate that while positive emotional connections are developed in those settings, there is little spiritual accountability that takes place there. In fact, only one out of every twenty churchgoers contends that he or she has any kind of church-based spiritual accountability in place. Small groups are the most common source of such engagement, but only 2 percent of all self-described Christians who attend church admit to having such accountability.

A significant challenge for churches is to have a plan for how meaningful community will be developed. Most small groups, as well as Christian education classes (e.g., Sunday school) focus on the transmission of information and the development and maintenance of faith-based relationships. Such gatherings do relatively well at accomplishing those goals. However, research indicates there is little difference in the faith and lifestyle of those who participate in such gatherings from those who don't. That shows that simply getting people to attend those meetings is not the solution.

There are numerous shortcomings related to this approach

— absence of genuine leadership, wishy-washy teaching, absence of accountability for application, disconnection from any larger transformational goals — that suggest continued reliance on such groups will not propel the Church forward. The current goal of tens of thousands of Protestant churches of getting more people to sign up for small groups will not reap much fruit for the kingdom.

The organized church could foster better outcomes but it will require leadership and measurable goals. What kinds of goals? Anecdotal evidence indicates that the following outcomes are achievable if an appropriate process and structure are put into place:

- *A clear purpose for the faith-based relationships.* Scripture notes the valuable role of community in helping us to see ourselves more clearly, even as a means of facilitating further transformation. [23] That outcome requires trust and vulnerability.

- *Connecting people by what stop they're on on the journey.* The dominant practice of conventional churches is to isolate men, women, teenagers and children into groups according to gender and age. Instead, what would happen if we teamed people according to their status on the journey? Would a greater level of learning and bonding take place than happens now? Several instances explored revealed that richer discussions happen because of the relevance of people's experiences to each others' lives.

- *Becoming a place of healing and celebration.* As noted throughout this book, the journey to wholeness is fraught with hardships and challenges. Each step forward creates a history of difficulties overcome and satisfying triumphs. What would happen if churches, perhaps through their smaller units, emphasized encouraging people to continue the journey and celebrating gains posted by each sojourner? Could the body of believers become a healing presence through their focused support, even more so than the positive but rather generic support presently delivered in most groups?

- *Prayer for growth on the journey.* The Church is called upon by Christ to intercede for the best interests of each other. Prayer happens in small groups. But what if, instead of prayers for job security, restored health, avoidance of hardships, and safe travel we were to relate our prayers to a person's transformation?

- *Adding accountability.* Small groups major on friendship and study. Those are benefits that should not be minimized or abandoned. But what about upping the ante on accountability? Rather than allowing it to be the tepid discussion of whether we have regularly attended church services, maintained our diets, and spoken kindly to those who have offended us, is it reasonable to expect that a spiritual *family* can lovingly and purposefully get in each other's face in order to promote genuine spiritual growth? If not, then should we disband these groups so that the pretense of accountability is not among our sins? Facilitating forms of authentic community is almost always beneficial. Upholding the pretense of community is detrimental to the spiritual well-being of those involved. Take a hard look at what you church is doing to provide interaction that supports each person's journey forward, rather than the church's image and traditions.

TRANSFORMATION AND LEADERSHIP

A group — whether it is a church, a baseball team, a corporation, a Bible study, or a family — cannot go beyond wherever its leaders take it. As we ponder the role of the local church and organic communities of faith in the transformation journey, we have to consider what leadership looks like in this context.

Regardless of the ministry model in place — a conventional church, a house church, an online community of faith, a marketplace gathering, a nuclear family — all leaders, whether professionally trained or not, paid or volunteer, fulltime or part-time — need to be immersed in their own transformational journey (and showing signs of consistent effort and growth). Making this a basic, non-negotiable requirement would automatically place greater emphasis upon the importance of transformation rather than upon less meaningful, more programmatic outcomes.

The role of senior pastor might also be reconstituted from that of dominant preacher to that of primary spiritual director. This will be a difficult, long-term transition to facilitate, since most pastors are well-educated and have been trained in skill areas that are not related to the classical spiritual disciplines. In other words, while knowledgeable and committed, many pastors have not gotten as far down the transformational pathway as would be desirable. Because you cannot give what you don't have, the people in their churches have suffered — knowledgeable but not deeply formed.

A significant step toward facilitating transformational outcomes would be to raise up families as the primary unit of ministry, rather than the congregation and its sub-units. This is both biblical and practical. To accomplish this end, church leaders would need to place the responsibility for spiritual development and transformation on the shoulders of the leaders of the family, empowering and enabling parents to provide spiritual leadership within the home and count on their community of faith for support.

And keeping in mind the importance of continual measurement and adjustment, leaders would do well to have transformation-based metrics in mind. When evaluating a potential course of action, the appropriate questions are to envision how that effort will advance people's journey to the heart of God, rather than how many new attenders will be attracted or the potential impact on fundraising.

Leaders set the stage and determine the pace of growth for those who follow them. Tinkering with the currently popular approaches that have proven to be inept at producing transformation will continue to put people's lives in harm's way.

TRANSFORMATION AND YOU

A revolution is built one person at a time. It starts with you. If you want to make a difference in the world, start with yourself.

This is the essence of Jesus's message where He taught that you should remove the plank from your eye before complaining to someone else about the speck in theirs. God will gladly use you as an instrument to change the world, but you must be the first alteration in that process. Once you become transformed, or at least demonstrably serious about being transformed by God, then you have some credibility for reaching out to others and show yourself to be worthy to be used in the lives of others. Until you get "down and dirty" in the process in your own life, you are simply a theorist. We don't need more of those.

If you believe that God wants you to be transformed, and you are willing to cooperate with Him to produce miraculous outcome, your courage and determination will not be wasted. As people see the impact God makes upon you throughout the journey, and as you convert your own journey into influence upon others, progress will be made.

The challenge is not so much up to a denomination or a church; it is up to you. If you will not accept God at His word and step out in faith to allow Him to reform your life, why should anyone else? And who will be to blame in the end? Not organizations and institutions, because we can never expect institutions to produce transformation. That's up to God and you.

.

ENDNOTES

1. These figures were found at http://imagine.gsfc.nasa.gov/docs/ask_astro/ answers/970401c.html.

2. Data on Boeing airplanes is provided at http://www.boeing.com/ commercial/747family/pf/pf_facts.html.

3. For a more extensive discussion of how God instills His vision in our hearts and longs for us to embrace that as our lifelong cause, see *The Cause within You*, by Matthew Barnett with George Barna, Tyndale Publishing, Carol Stream, IL, 2011. Grasping how vision works is also discussed in practical terms in *The Power of Vision*, by George Barna, Regal Books, Ventura, CA, 1992.

4. While the entire conversation that Jesus had was geared to transforming people's lives — His Sermon on the Mount, alone, is a mind-boggling rewriting of the plan for our lives — simple verses that encapsulate this thinking are found in Galatians 6:15 and Romans 12:2.

5. I am well aware that the context of this passage addresses judgment, not assisting others in their spiritual development. However, the principle underlying this passage is relevant: avoid the hypocrisy of trying to shape others into something that you have not yet experienced.

6. See Matthew 7:15-20, 12:33-37, 21:43; John 15:1-17; Luke 3:8-9, 13:1-9; Romans 1:13, 7:4-6; Philippians 1:9-11; Colossians 1:6, 10; and James 3:17.

7. Matthew 7:21-23.

8. For each of these 29 outcomes there are numerous verses and passages to consider. Here are a few to get you started. *Trustworthy servants*: Matthew 6:1-4, 12:11-12, 20:24-28, 24:14-46, John 9:4, 13:12-17. *Becoming genuine followers of Christ*: Matthew 4:19, 8:22, 16:24-25, 19:21, 28; Mark 2:14;

John 6:29, 8:12, 31-32, 10:27, 12:25-26, 15:1-8, 21:19,22. *Obedient, holy*: Matthew 5:8, 28:20; Luke 8:21, 11:28; John 5:14, 8:51, 14:15, 21, 23-24, 17:14-19. *Lovers of people*: Matthew 5:43-47; Mark 12:31, John 13:34-35, 15:12, 17. *Lovers of God*: Matthew 10:37-39; Mark 12:30. *Evangelizers*: Matthew 4:19, 10:32, 28:19-20. *Peacemakers*: Matthew 5:9. *Being a person of abundant faith*: Matthew 9:29, 14:22-31, 15:21-28, 17:14-21, 21: 21-22, 23:23, Luke 18:42-43; John 5:24, 14:1-4. *Fearless believer*: Matthew 10:16-20, 26-31; 24:9-13. *Student of the Bible*: Matthew 13:12, 22:32; John 17:6-8. *Being a passionate worshipper of God*: Matthew 26:6-13; Luke 4:8, 16:13, 19:36-40, 22:14-20; John 4:23-24, 12:27-28. *Humble*: Matthew 5:5, 18:4, 23:8-12, Luke 17:7-10, 22:24-27. *Being a godly role model*: Matthew 18:5-9. *Forgiving*: Matthew 6:14-15, 18:21-22, Luke 15:11-32, 17:3-4, 23:34. *Seeking justice*: Matthew 5:6, 18:23-35, 23:23, Luke 18:2-8. *Being merciful*: Matthew 5:7, 23:23. *Becoming a person of integrity*: Matthew 23:27-28, Luke 16:10-12. *Prayer warrior*: Matthew 6:6-13, 26:41, Luke 22:40, John 16:24. *Pursuing God's will*: Matthew 26:42. *Supporting the needy*: Luke 12:33. *Being continually repentant*: Luke 13:1-5, 18:13-14; John 3:1-21. *Grateful recipient of God's gifts*: Luke 17:17-18. *Generous steward*: Luke 21:1-4. *Morally alert and blameless*: Luke 21:34-36. *At peace with life*: John 14:27. *Joyful*: John 15:11, 16:24. *Friend of Jesus*: John 15:15. *Persecuted believer*: Matthew 5:10, John 15:18-27, 17:14-18. *Lover of truth*: John 17:17, 18:37.

9. New Testament references to becoming holy include Romans 1:7, 6:19; 1 Corinthians 1:2; Ephesians 1:1, 1:18, 4:24; Colossians 3:12; Hebrews 10:10, 10:29. We are exhorted to imitate God in Ephesians 5:1. Jesus called His followers to be the light of the world in the Sermon on the Mount, Matthew 5:14.

10. Luke 14:25-35.

11. "National Study Describes Christian Accountability Provided by Churches," Barna Group, November 29, 2010, http://www.barna.org/congregations-articles/454-study-describes-christian-accountability-provided-by-churches.

12. This is based on a national survey conducted among self-defined Christians. Among individuals who were in the advanced stops on the

journey — Stop 9 or higher — 51% had undergone one of the life crises mentioned and credited it with moving them into a serious pursuit of God.

13. Tozer, A.W. *The Pursuit of God*. Camp Hill, PA: Christian Publications. 1982.

14. Kreeft, Peter (Editor). *Summa of the Summa*. San Francisco: Ignatius Press. 1990.

15. 1 Corinthians 13:13-14:1.

16. http://www.quotes.net/quote/66.

17. For examples of such fasting, see Ezra 8:21-23 and 2Samuel 12.

18. I realize there are at least 45 instances where the New Testament indicates we are to do something positive for each other. However, many of those passages have overlapping content, thus reducing the aggregate number of behaviors commended to us. For instance, there are at least 11 passages that tell us to love one another. In stating that we have about 25 commands to follow in our treatment of each other, I am speaking about the unique behaviors provided in those four dozen or so passages.

19. The command to love each other is expressed in its variations in Philippians 2:2; 1 Thessalonians 4:9, 5:13; Hebrews 13:1; 1 Peter 1:22, 3:8, 4:8, 5:14; 1 John 3:18, 4:11-12, 4:19; Romans 12:10, 12:16, 14:19, 15:5, 15:7; 1 Corinthians 1:10, 3:3, 12:25; Ephesians 4:2, 4:32; and 1 John 1:7.

20. See Hebrews 3:13.

21. Instances of calling us to support, enhance and assist in each other's growth occur in Romans 14:19, 15:32; 1 Thessalonians 4:8, 5:11, 5:15; Jude 1:20;2 Corinthians 13:11; 1 Corinthians 12:7; Colossians 3:16; Hebrews 12:15; and James 5:16.

22. Advancing each other through trust and respect is commanded in 1 Corinthians 3:3; Philippians 2:2; Ephesians 4:32; Colossians 3:9; James 4:11, 5:9, 5:16; Romans 12:10, 14:13; 1 Peter 3:8, 5:5.

23. See Proverb 27:6.

APPENDICES

SCRIPTURES FOR REFLECTION

SELECTED PASSAGES REGARDING TRANSFORMATION

Don't copy the behavior and customs of this world, but let God transform you into a new person by changing the way you think. Then you will learn to know God's will for you, which is good and pleasing and perfect. — Romans 12:2

This means that anyone who belongs to Christ has become a new person. The old life is gone; a new life has begun! — 2 Corinthians 5:17

It doesn't matter whether we have been circumcised or not. What counts is whether we have been transformed into a new creation. — Galatians 6:15

Instead, let the Spirit renew your thoughts and attitudes. Put on your new nature, created to be like God — truly righteous and holy. — Ephesians 4:23-24

SELECTED PASSAGES REGARDING SALVATION

"Not everyone who calls out to me, 'Lord! Lord!' will enter the Kingdom of Heaven. Only those who actually do the will of my Father in heaven will enter. On judgment day many will say to me, 'Lord! Lord! We prophesied in your name and cast out demons in your name and performed many miracles in your name.' But I will reply, 'I never knew you. Get away from me, you who break God's laws.'" — Matthew 7:21-23

And then he told them, "Go into all the world and preach the Good News to everyone. Anyone who believes and is baptized will be saved. But anyone who refuses to believe will be condemned. These miraculous signs will accompany those who believe: They will cast out demons in my name, and they will speak in new languages." — Mark 16:15-17

One day Jesus told a story in the form of a parable to a large crowd that had gathered from many towns to hear him: "A farmer went out to plant his seed. As he scattered it across his field, some seed fell on a footpath, where it was stepped on, and the birds ate it. Other seed fell among rocks. It began to grow, but the plant soon wilted and died for lack of moisture. Other seed fell among thorns that grew up with it and choked out the tender plants. Still other seed fell on fertile soil. This seed grew and produced a crop that was a hundred times as much as had been planted!" When he had said this, he called out, "Anyone with ears to hear should listen and understand." His disciples asked him what this parable meant. He replied, "You are permitted to understand the secrets of the Kingdom of God. But I use parables to teach the others so that the Scriptures might be fulfilled: 'When they look, they won't really see. When they hear, they won't understand.' This is the meaning of the parable: The seed is God's word. The seeds that fell on the footpath represent those who hear the message, only to have the devil come and take it away from their hearts and prevent them from believing and being saved. The seeds on the rocky soil represent those who hear the message and receive it with joy. But since they don't have deep roots, they believe for a while, then they fall away when they face temptation. The seeds that fell among the thorns represent those who hear the message, but all too quickly the message is crowded out by the cares and riches and pleasures of this life. And so they never grow into maturity. And the seeds that fell on the good soil represent honest, good-hearted people who hear God's word, cling to it, and patiently produce a huge harvest. — Luke 8:4-15

"So let everyone in Israel know for certain that God has made this Jesus, whom you crucified, to be both Lord and Messiah!" Peter's words pierced their hearts, and they said to him and to the other apostles, "Brothers, what should we do?" Peter replied, "Each of you must repent of your sins and turn to God, and be baptized in the name of Jesus Christ for the

forgiveness of your sins. Then you will receive the gift of the Holy Spirit. This promise is to you, and to your children, and even to the Gentiles — all who have been called by the Lord our God." — Acts 2:36-39

For Jesus is the one referred to in the Scriptures, where it says, "The stone that you builders rejected has now become the cornerstone." There is salvation in no one else! God has given no other name under heaven by which we must be saved. — Acts 4:11-12

We believe that we are all saved the same way, by the undeserved grace of the Lord Jesus. — Acts 15:11

When you were slaves to sin, you were free from the obligation to do right. And what was the result? You are now ashamed of the things you used to do, things that end in eternal doom. But now you are free from the power of sin and have become slaves of God. Now you do those things that lead to holiness and result in eternal life. For the wages of sin is death, but the free gift of God is eternal life through Christ Jesus our Lord. — Romans 6:20-23

If you confess with your mouth that Jesus is Lord and believe in your heart that God raised him from the dead, you will be saved. For it is by believing in your heart that you are made right with God, and it is by confessing with your mouth that you are saved... For "Everyone who calls on the name of the Lord will be saved." — Romans 10:9-10, 13

But those who depend on the law to make them right with God are under his curse, for the Scriptures say, "Cursed is everyone who does not observe and obey all the commands that are written in God's Book of the Law." So it is clear that no one can be made right with God by trying to keep the law. For the Scriptures say, "It is through faith that a righteous person has life." — Galatians 3:10-11

Once you were dead because of your disobedience and your many sins. You used to live in sin, just like the rest of the world, obeying the devil — the commander of the powers in the unseen world. He is the spirit at work in the hearts of those who refuse to obey God. All of us used to live that way, following the passionate desires and inclinations of our sinful nature. By our very nature we were subject to God's anger, just like everyone else. But God is so rich in mercy, and he loved us so much, that even though we were dead because of our sins, he gave us life when he raised Christ from the dead. (It is only by God's grace that you have been saved!) For he raised us from the dead along with Christ and seated us with him in the heavenly realms because we are united with Christ Jesus. So God can point to us in all future ages as examples of the incredible wealth of his grace and kindness toward us, as shown in all he has done for us who are united with Christ Jesus. God saved you by his grace when you believed. And you can't take credit for this; it is a gift from God. Salvation is not a reward for the good things we have done, so none of us can boast about it. For we are God's masterpiece. He has created us anew in Christ Jesus, so we can do the good things he planned for us long ago. — Ephesians 2:1-10

For you know that God paid a ransom to save you from the empty life you inherited from your ancestors. And the ransom he paid was not mere gold or silver. It was the precious blood of Christ, the sinless, spotless Lamb of God. God chose him as your ransom long before the world began, but he has now revealed him to you in these last days. Through Christ you have come to trust in God. And you have placed your faith and hope in God because he raised Christ from the dead and gave him great glory. You were cleansed from your sins when you obeyed the truth, so now you must show sincere love to each other as brothers and sisters. Love each other deeply with all your heart. For you have been born again, but not to a life that will quickly end. Your new life will last forever because it comes from the eternal, living word of God. — 1 Peter 1:18-23

God showed how much he loved us by sending his one and only Son into the world so that we might have eternal life through him. This is real love — not that we loved God, but that he loved us and sent his Son as a sacrifice to take away our sins. — 1 John 4:9-10

SELECTED PASSAGES ABOUT HOLINESS

So set yourselves apart to be holy, for I am the Lord your God. Keep all my decrees by putting them into practice, for I am the Lord who makes you holy. — Leviticus 20:7-8

You must be holy because I, the Lord, am holy. I have set you apart from all other people to be my very own. — Leviticus 20:26

Make them holy by your truth; teach them your word, which is truth. Just as you sent me into the world, I am sending them into the world. And I give myself as a holy sacrifice for them so they can be made holy by your truth. — John 17:17-19

I am writing to God's church in Corinth, to you who have been called by God to be his own holy people. He made you holy by means of Christ Jesus, just as he did for all people everywhere who call on the name of our Lord Jesus Christ, their Lord and ours. — 1 Corinthians 1:2

Put on your new nature, created to be like God — truly righteous and holy. — Ephesians 4:24

This includes you who were once far away from God. You were his enemies, separated from him by your evil thoughts and actions. Yet now he has reconciled you to himself through the death of Christ in his physical body. As a result, he has brought you into his own presence, and you are holy and blameless as you stand before him without a single fault. — Colossians 1:21-22

Since God chose you to be the holy people he loves, you must clothe yourselves with tenderhearted mercy, kindness, humility, gentleness, and patience. — Colossians 3:12

For God saved us and called us to live a holy life. He did this, not because we deserved it, but because that was his plan from before the beginning of time — to show us his grace through Christ Jesus. — 2 Timothy 1:9

God the Father knew you and chose you long ago, and his Spirit has made you holy. — 1 Peter 1:2

Blessed and holy are those who share in the first resurrection. For them the second death holds no power, but they will be priests of God and of Christ and will reign with him a thousand years. — Revelation 20:6

SELECTED PASSAGES REGARDING BROKENNESS

Then Nathan said to David, "You are that man! The Lord, the God of Israel, says: I anointed you king of Israel and saved you from the power of Saul. I gave you your master's house and his wives and the kingdoms of Israel and Judah. And if that had not been enough, I would have given you much, much more. Why, then, have you despised the word of the Lord and done this horrible deed? For you have murdered Uriah the Hittite with the sword of the Ammonites and stolen his wife. From this time on, your family will live by the sword because you have despised me by taking Uriah's wife to be your own. This is what the Lord says: Because of what you have done, I will cause your own household to rebel against you. I will give your wives to another man before your very eyes, and he will go to bed with them in public view. You did it secretly, but I will make this happen to you openly in the sight of all Israel." Then David confessed to Nathan, "I have sinned against the Lord." Nathan replied, "Yes, but the Lord has forgiven you, and you won't die for this sin. Nevertheless, because you have shown utter contempt for the Lord by doing this, your child will die." After Nathan returned to his home, the Lord sent a deadly illness to the child of David and Uriah's wife. — 2 Samuel 12:7-15

Then Jesus went with them to the olive grove called Gethsemane, and he said, "Sit here while I go over there to pray." He took Peter and Zebedee's two sons, James and John, and he became anguished and distressed. He told them, "My soul is crushed with grief to the point of death. Stay here and keep watch with me." He went on a little farther and bowed with his face to the ground, praying, "My Father! If it is possible, let this cup of suffering be taken away from me. Yet I want your will to be done, not mine." Then he returned to the disciples and found them asleep. He said to Peter, "Couldn't you watch with me even one hour? Keep watch and pray, so that you will not give in to temptation. For the spirit is willing, but the body is weak!" Then Jesus left them a second time and prayed, "My Father! If this cup cannot be taken away unless I drink it, your will be done." When he returned to them again, he found them sleeping, for they couldn't keep their eyes open. So he went to pray a third time, saying the same things again. Then he came to the disciples and said, "Go ahead and sleep. Have your rest. But look — the time has come. The Son of Man is betrayed into the hands of sinners. Up, let's be going. Look, my betrayer is here!"... Then the people who had arrested Jesus led him to the home of Caiaphas, the high priest, where the teachers of religious law and the elders had gathered. Meanwhile, Peter followed him at a distance and came to the high priest's courtyard. He went in and sat with the guards and waited to see how it would all end. Inside, the leading priests and the entire high council were trying to find witnesses who would lie about Jesus, so they could put him to death. But even though they found many who agreed to give false witness, they could not use anyone's testimony. Finally, two men came forward who declared, "This man said, 'I am able to destroy the Temple of God and rebuild it in three days.'" Then the high priest stood up and said to Jesus, "Well, aren't you going to answer these charges? What do you have to say for yourself?" But Jesus remained silent. Then the high priest said to him, "I demand in the name of the living God — tell us if you are the Messiah, the Son of God." Jesus replied, "You have said it. And in the future you will see the Son of Man seated in the place of power at God's right hand and coming on the clouds of heaven." Then the high priest tore his clothing to show his horror and said, "Blasphemy! Why do we need other witnesses?

You have all heard his blasphemy. What is your verdict?" "Guilty!" they shouted. "He deserves to die!" Then they began to spit in Jesus' face and beat him with their fists. And some slapped him, jeering, "Prophesy to us, you Messiah! Who hit you that time?" Meanwhile, Peter was sitting outside in the courtyard. A servant girl came over and said to him, "You were one of those with Jesus the Galilean." But Peter denied it in front of everyone. "I don't know what you're talking about," he said. Later, out by the gate, another servant girl noticed him and said to those standing around, "This man was with Jesus of Nazareth." Again Peter denied it, this time with an oath. "I don't even know the man," he said. A little later some of the other bystanders came over to Peter and said, "You must be one of them; we can tell by your Galilean accent." Peter swore, "A curse on me if I'm lying — I don't know the man!" And immediately the rooster crowed. Suddenly, Jesus' words flashed through Peter's mind: "Before the rooster crows, you will deny three times that you even know me." And he went away, weeping bitterly. — Matthew 26:36-46, 57-75

Meanwhile, Saul was uttering threats with every breath and was eager to kill the Lord's followers. So he went to the high priest. He requested letters addressed to the synagogues in Damascus, asking for their co-operation in the arrest of any followers of the Way he found there. He wanted to bring them — both men and women — back to Jerusalem in chains. As he was approaching Damascus on this mission, a light from heaven suddenly shone down around him. He fell to the ground and heard a voice saying to him, "Saul! Saul! Why are you persecuting me?" "Who are you, lord?" Saul asked. And the voice replied, "I am Jesus, the one you are persecuting! Now get up and go into the city, and you will be told what you must do." The men with Saul stood speechless, for they heard the sound of someone's voice but saw no one! Saul picked himself up off the ground, but when he opened his eyes he was blind. So his companions led him by the hand to Damascus. He remained there blind for three days and did not eat or drink. — Acts 9:1-9

SELECTED PASSAGES REGARDING SURRENDER/SUBMISSION

Do not be like your ancestors and relatives who abandoned the Lord, the God of their ancestors, and became an object of derision, as you yourselves can see. Do not be stubborn, as they were, but submit yourselves to the Lord. Come to his Temple, which he has set apart as holy forever. Worship the Lord your God so that his fierce anger will turn away from you. — 2 Chronicles 30:7-8

Trust in the Lord with all your heart; do not depend on your own understanding. Seek his will in all you do, and he will show you which path to take. — Proverbs 3:5-6

The Sovereign Lord has spoken to me, and I have listened. I have not rebelled or turned away. I offered my back to those who beat me and my cheeks to those who pulled out my beard. I did not hide my face from mockery and spitting. Because the Sovereign Lord helps me, I will not be disgraced. Therefore, I have set my face like a stone, determined to do his will. And I know that I will not be put to shame. — Isaiah 50:5-7

So it is good to wait quietly for salvation from the Lord. And it is good for people to submit at an early age to the yoke of his discipline: Let them sit alone in silence beneath the Lord's demands. — Lamentations 3:26-28

"But among you it will be different. Whoever wants to be a leader among you must be your servant, and whoever wants to be first among you must be the slave of everyone else. For even the Son of Man came not to be served but to serve others and to give his life as a ransom for many." — Mark 10:43-45

A large crowd was following Jesus. He turned around and said to them, "If you want to be my disciple, you must hate everyone else by comparison — your father and mother, wife and children, brothers and sisters — yes, even your own life. Otherwise, you cannot be my disciple. And if you do not carry your own cross and follow me, you cannot be my dis-

ciple... So you cannot become my disciple without giving up everything you own." — Luke 14:25-27, 33

They called in the apostles and had them flogged. Then they ordered them never again to speak in the name of Jesus, and they let them go. The apostles left the high council rejoicing that God had counted them worthy to suffer disgrace for the name of Jesus. And every day, in the Temple and from house to house, they continued to teach and preach this message: "Jesus is the Messiah." — Acts 5:40-42

So you also should consider yourselves to be dead to the power of sin and alive to God through Christ Jesus. Do not let sin control the way you live; do not give in to sinful desires. Do not let any part of your body become an instrument of evil to serve sin. Instead, give yourselves completely to God, for you were dead, but now you have new life. So use your whole body as an instrument to do what is right for the glory of God. — Romans 6:11-13

Well then, since God's grace has set us free from the law, does that mean we can go on sinning? Of course not! Don't you realize that you become the slave of whatever you choose to obey? You can be a slave to sin, which leads to death, or you can choose to obey God, which leads to righteous living. Thank God! Once you were slaves of sin, but now you wholeheartedly obey this teaching we have given you. — Romans 6:15-17

Those who are dominated by the sinful nature think about sinful things, but those who are controlled by the Holy Spirit think about things that please the Spirit. So letting your sinful nature control your mind leads to death. But letting the Spirit control your mind leads to life and peace. For the sinful nature is always hostile to God. It never did obey God's laws, and it never will. That's why those who are still under the control of their sinful nature can never please God. But you are not controlled by your sinful nature. You are controlled by the Spirit if you have the Spirit of God living in you. — Romans 8:5-9

And do not bring sorrow to God's Holy Spirit by the way you live.

Remember, he has identified you as his own, guaranteeing that you will be saved on the day of redemption. — Ephesians 4:30

For you have been given not only the privilege of trusting in Christ but also the privilege of suffering for him. — Philippians 1:29

So do not throw away this confident trust in the Lord. Remember the great reward it brings you! Patient endurance is what you need now, so that you will continue to do God's will. Then you will receive all that he has promised. — Hebrews 10:35-36

So then, since Christ suffered physical pain, you must arm yourselves with the same attitude he had, and be ready to suffer, too. For if you have suffered physically for Christ, you have finished with sin. You won't spend the rest of your lives chasing your own desires, but you will be anxious to do the will of God. — 1 Peter 4:1-2

SELECTED PASSAGES ABOUT LOVING GOD

Then God gave the people all these instructions: "I am the Lord your God, who rescued you from the land of Egypt, the place of your slavery. You must not have any other god but me. You must not make for yourself an idol of any kind or an image of anything in the heavens or on the earth or in the sea. You must not bow down to them or worship them, for I, the Lord your God, am a jealous God who will not tolerate your affection for any other gods. I lay the sins of the parents upon their children; the entire family is affected — even children in the third and fourth generations of those who reject me. But I lavish unfailing love for a thousand generations on those who love me and obey my commands." — Exodus 20:1-6

But be very careful to obey all the commands and the instructions that Moses gave to you. Love the Lord your God, walk in all his ways, obey his commands, hold firmly to him, and serve him with all your heart and all your soul. — Joshua 22:5

So be very careful to love the LORD your God. — Joshua 23:11

Love the LORD, all you godly ones! For the LORD protects those who are loyal to him, but he harshly punishes the arrogant. — Psalm 31:23

One of the teachers of religious law was standing there listening to the debate. He realized that Jesus had answered well, so he asked, "Of all the commandments, which is the most important?" Jesus replied, "The most important commandment is this: 'Listen, O Israel! The LORD our God is the one and only LORD. And you must love the LORD your God with all your heart, all your soul, all your mind, and all your strength." — Mark 12:28-30

"I have loved you even as the Father has loved me. Remain in my love. When you obey my commandments, you remain in my love, just as I obey my Father's commandments and remain in his love. I have told you these things so that you will be filled with my joy. Yes, your joy will overflow!" — John 15:9-11

"You are my friends if you do what I command. I no longer call you slaves, because a master doesn't confide in his slaves. Now you are my friends, since I have told you everything the Father told me." — John 15:14-15

SELECTED PASSAGES ABOUT LOVING PEOPLE

Do not seek revenge or bear a grudge against a fellow Israelite, but love your neighbor as yourself. — Leviticus 19:18

"This is my commandment: Love each other in the same way I have loved you." — John 15:12

Don't just pretend to love others. Really love them. Hate what is wrong. Hold tightly to what is good. Love each other with genuine affection, and take delight in honoring each other. — Romans 12:9-10

May God, who gives this patience and encouragement, help you live in complete harmony with each other, as is fitting for followers of Christ

Jesus. Then all of you can join together with one voice, giving praise and glory to God, the Father of our Lord Jesus Christ. Therefore, accept each other just as Christ has accepted you so that God will be given glory. — Romans 15:5-7

This makes for harmony among the members, so that all the members care for each other. If one part suffers, all the parts suffer with it, and if one part is honored, all the parts are glad. All of you together are Christ's body, and each of you is a part of it. — 1 Corinthians 12:25-27

Get rid of all bitterness, rage, anger, harsh words, and slander, as well as all types of evil behavior. Instead, be kind to each other, tenderhearted, forgiving one another, just as God through Christ has forgiven you. — Ephesians 4:31- 32

Then make me truly happy by agreeing wholeheartedly with each other, loving one another, and working together with one mind and purpose. — Philippians 2:2

You were cleansed from your sins when you obeyed the truth, so now you must show sincere love to each other as brothers and sisters. Love each other deeply with all your heart. — 1 Peter 1:22

Dear children, let's not merely say that we love each other; let us show the truth by our actions. — 1 John 3:18

Dear friends, since God loved us that much, we surely ought to love each other. No one has ever seen God. But if we love each other, God lives in us, and his love is brought to full expression in us. — 1 John 4:11-12

We love each other because he loved us first. If someone says, "I love God," but hates a Christian brother or sister, that person is a liar; for if we don't love people we can see, how can we love God, whom we cannot see? — 1 John 4:19-20

SELECTED PASSAGES REGARDING BEARING FRUIT

"Prove by the way you live that you have repented of your sins and turned to God. Don't just say to each other, 'We're safe, for we are descendants of Abraham.' That means nothing, for I tell you, God can create children of Abraham from these very stones. Even now the ax of God's judgment is poised, ready to sever the roots of the trees. Yes, every tree that does not produce good fruit will be chopped down and thrown into the fire."
— Luke 3:8-9

I want to work among you and see spiritual fruit, just as I have seen among other Gentiles. — Romans 1:13

"Beware of false prophets who come disguised as harmless sheep but are really vicious wolves. You can identify them by their fruit, that is, by the way they act. Can you pick grapes from thornbushes, or figs from thistles? A good tree produces good fruit, and a bad tree produces bad fruit. A good tree can't produce bad fruit, and a bad tree can't produce good fruit. So every tree that does not produce good fruit is chopped down and thrown into the fire. Yes, just as you can identify a tree by its fruit, so you can identify people by their actions." – Matthew 7:15-20

"A tree is identified by its fruit. If a tree is good, its fruit will be good. If a tree is bad, its fruit will be bad. You brood of snakes! How could evil men like you speak what is good and right? For whatever is in your heart determines what you say. A good person produces good things from the treasury of a good heart, and an evil person produces evil things from the treasury of an evil heart." — Matthew 12:33-35

"I am the true grapevine, and my Father is the gardener. He cuts off every branch of mine that doesn't produce fruit, and he prunes the branches that do bear fruit so they will produce even more. You have already been pruned and purified by the message I have given you. Remain in me, and I will remain in you. For a branch cannot produce fruit if it is severed from the vine, and you cannot be fruitful unless you remain in me. Yes, I am the vine; you are the branches. Those who remain in me, and I

in them, will produce much fruit. For apart from me you can do nothing. Anyone who does not remain in me is thrown away like a useless branch and withers. Such branches are gathered into a pile to be burned. But if you remain in me and my words remain in you, you may ask for anything you want, and it will be granted! When you produce much fruit, you are my true disciples. This brings great glory to my Father." — John 15:1-8

May you always be filled with the fruit of your salvation — the righteous character produced in your life by Jesus Christ — for this will bring much glory and praise to God. — Philippians 1:11

So we have not stopped praying for you since we first heard about you. We ask God to give you complete knowledge of his will and to give you spiritual wisdom and understanding. Then the way you live will always honor and please the Lord, and your lives will produce every kind of good fruit. All the while, you will grow as you learn to know God better and better. — Colossians 1:9-10

If you are wise and understand God's ways, prove it by living an honorable life, doing good works with the humility that comes from wisdom. — James 3:13

MAXIMIZING YOUR FAITH

Maximum Faith: Live Like Jesus is more than just a book. The team behind the book prays that God will use this publication as a catalyst to a movement of God's people who are not willing to settle for routines and rules but who want to fully devote their life to God and become all that He wants them to be.

Additional resources have been and will continue to be created to help serious followers of Christ build and maintain momentum on their journey to holiness. Those resources, which will be released throughout 2011 and 2012, will include instructional DVDs, a small group curriculum, worship songs related to each of the stops on the journey, a website with various tools for growth, live ministry events, diagnostic tools, and more.

To take advantage of the resources that are of greatest interest and value to you, stay in touch with the Maximum Faith team through our websites:

www.maximumfaith.com

www.georgebarna.com

To contact George Barna regarding transformation and Maximum Faith ministry, email: george@georgebarna.com

BIBLIOGRAPHY

Allen, Diogenes. *Spiritual Theology.* Lanham, MD: Cowley Publications. 1997.

Barna, George. *Futurecast.* Carol Stream, IL: Tyndale House Publishers. 2011.

———. *The Seven Faith Tribes.* Carol Stream, IL: Tyndale House Publishers. 2009.

———. *Revolutionary Parenting.* Carol Stream, IL: Tyndale House Publishers. 2007.

———. *Revolution.* Carol Stream, IL: Tyndale House Publishers. 2005.

———. *Think Like Jesus.* Nashville: Integrity Publishers. 2003.

———. *Transforming Children into Spiritual Champions.* Ventura, CA: Regal Books. 2003.

Bruce, Barbara. *Our Spiritual Brain.* Nashville: Abingdon Press. 2002.

Colson, Charles and Harold Fickett. *The Faith.* Grand Rapids, MI: Zondervan. 2008.

Demarest, Bruce. *Seasons of the Soul.* Downers Grove, IL: InterVarsity Press. 2009.

DeMoss, Nancy. *Brokenness.* Chicago: Moody Press. 2002.

Feldmeier, Peter. *The Developing Christian.* Mahwah, NJ: Paulist Press. 2007.

Fletcher, William. *The Triumph of Surrender.* Colorado Springs, CO: NavPress. 1987.

Foster, Richard and Gayle Beebe. *Longing for God.* Downers Grove, IL: InterVarsity Press. 2009.

Foster, Richard. *Celebration of Discipline.* San Francisco: Harper San Francisco. 1998.

Fowler, James. *Becoming Adult, Becoming Christian*. San Francisco: Harper & Row. 1984.

———. *Faithful Change*. Nashville: Abingdon Press. 1996.

Freeman, Andy and Pete Greig. *Punk Monk*. Ventura, CA: Regal Books. 2007.

Kempis, Thomas A. *Of the Imitation of Christ*. New York: Walker and Company. 1987.

Kreeft, Peter (editor). *Summa of the Summa*. San Francisco: Ignatius Press. 1990.

Kreider, Larry. *Speak Lord, I'm Listening*. Ventura, CA: Regal Books. 2008.

Lawrence, Brother. *The Practice of the Presence of God*. Old Tappan, NJ: Fleming Revell. 1999.

Lawrenz, Mel. *The Dynamics of Spiritual Formation*. Grand Rapids, MI: Baker Books. 2000.

Manning, Brennan. *The Ragamuffin Gospel*. Sisters, OR: Multnomah Press. 2000.

Mannoia, Kevin and Don Thorsen (editors). *The Holiness Manifesto*. Grand Rapids, MI: Eerdmans Publishing. 2008.

Merton, Thomas. *The Wisdom of the Desert*. New York: New Directions Publishing. 1960.

Murray, Andrew. *Absolute Surrender*. Springdale, PA: Whitaker House. 1982.

Norris, Kathleen. *The Cloister Walk*. New York: Riverhead Books. 1996.

Nouwen, Henri. *Spiritual Direction*. New York: HarperOne. 2006.

———. *Life of the Beloved*. New York: Crossroad Publishing. 1992.

Oden, Thomas. *The Transforming Power of Grace*. Nashville: Abingdon Press. 1993.

Olukoya, D.K. *Dealing with Unprofitable Roots*. Nigeria: Mountain of Fire and Miracles Ministries. 1999.

Ortberg, John. *The Me I Want to Be*. Grand Rapids, MI: Zondervan. 2010.

———. *The Life You've Always Wanted*. Grand Rapids, MI: Zondervan. 2002.

Ryan, Thomas. *Disciplines for Christian Living*. Mahwah, NJ: Paulist Press. 1993.

Ryle, J.C. *Holiness*. Wheaton, IL: Billy Graham Center. 1996.

Saunders, Monroe. *Transformational Spiritual Development in Leadership and Congregational Development*. Dayton, OH: United Theological Seminary. 2004.

Tozer, A.W. *The Pursuit of God*. Camp Hill, PA: Christian Publications. 1982.

———. *Experiencing the Presence of God*. Ventura, CA: Regal Books. 2010.

———. *Living As a Christian*. Ventura, CA: Regal Books. 2009.

Wagner, C. Peter. *Radical Holiness for Radical Living*. Colorado Springs, CO: Wagner Institute, 1998.

Wicks, Robert. *Living a Gentle, Passionate Life*. Mahwah, NJ: Paulist Press. 1998.

Willard, Dallas. *The Spirit of the Disciplines*. San Francisco: Harper & Row. 1988.

Willard, Dallas and Jan Johnson. *Renovation of the Heart in Daily Practice*. Colorado Springs, CO: NavPress. 2006.

Willard, Dallas, and Don Simpson. *Revolution of Character*. Colorado Springs, CO: NavPress. 2005.

ACKNOWLEDGEMENTS

I owe a lot of people my sincere thanks for their help with this book.

Many people helped with the research. Paul Braun of Braun Research fielded the studies and was very generous to me. That generosity enabled the research project to be completed more robustly than would otherwise have been possible. David Kinnaman and Pam Jacob of The Barna Group also significantly assisted with the research. Monique Reidy provided assistance with the secondary research that helped get things off the ground at the beginning stage of the project.

The content of this book is far superior to its original contours thanks to the feedback of those who read drafts of the manuscript at various stages in its development. Their comments helped redirect some of my wayward thinking and stray prose. Among those whose input was most helpful were Esther Fedorkevich, Brant Gerckens, Terry Gorka, Tom Johnson, Kevin Mannoia, Steve Russo, and John Saucier. Additional feedback and ideas were offered by Steve Carlock, Britt Merrick, and my friends at Tyndale Publishing.

An entire team of people traveled to Los Angeles at their own expense to help me develop the means of conveying and distributing this information to the people who need it or are likely to use it. Our common dream is that the Lord will use these insights to motivate a transformational movement in America. Besides some of the people mentioned above, the participants included Matthew Barnett, Michael Clifford, Bill Dallas, Kay Hiramine, Brad Matthias, and Gunnar Simonsen. The conclave was led by my partners in the Strategenius Group: Connie DeBord, Robert Hawkins, and Joel Tucciarone.

Converting this project into something usable has been a long and tortured process. I am especially grateful for the assistance of Anita Palmer of The Strong Word Communication Services for shaping the manuscript, significantly enhancing Jennifer's story, and overseeing the numerous publishing details.

Last but never least is my family. They have been a source of encouragement and have surrendered days of my time and attention as a way of supporting me and advancing the kingdom through this project. My wife Nancy, in particular, was understanding and supportive, accepting a double parenting burden while I squirreled away in my office to concentrate on how God does the miracle of transformation.

As always, I am humbled that God loves me, has saved me, gave me gifts and opportunities to serve, and has allowed me to write this book. I pray that He can find ways to use it to advance His kingdom and that this effort is a gift He finds pleasing.

All of the mistakes, bad ideas, dubious conclusions, and tortured English contained in these pages are my fault. The people listed above did their best to help, but there is only so much an adviser can do.

ABOUT THE RESEARCH

Throughout this book you will read about research that is not directly footnoted. Those statistics and data-based statements have been derived from a series of national public opinion surveys conducted by The Barna Group in relation to the Maximum Faith Project between 2005 and 2010. Those studies built on findings from two decades of national studies conducted prior to that time.

These surveys were conducted by telephone, with a special effort made to include people who no longer have a landline in their home but now rely solely on mobile telephones. Each survey—with one exception—involved a minimum of 1,000 people randomly selected from across the 48 continental states. The exception to that was a smaller survey conducted in 2009 among 400 self-described Christians.

All of the following studies were conducted among national random samples of adults (defined as people 18 or older). Upon completion of each survey, minimal statistical weights were applied to the data to allow the results to more closely correspond to known national demographic averages for several variables. In all of the surveys conducted since 2008, the sample universe included a sub-sample of people drawn from cell-phone households. All studies relied on callbacks to households not reached after the first attempt; a maximum of six callbacks were made to each nonresponsive household, with contact attempts made at different times of the day and days of the week. The average length of the surveys in these studies ranged from fifteen to twenty-two minutes.

◆　◆　◆　◆　◆

Study Identifier	Field Date	Sample Size	Maximum Sampling Error
OmniPoll™ 2-10	August 2010	1,000	± 3.2 percentage points
OmniPoll™ W-10	February 2010	1,005	± 3.2 percentage points
OmniPoll™ 1-10	February 2010	1,001	± 3.2 percentage points
Transformation GB-1	December 2009	400	± 5.0 percentage points
OmniPoll™ F-09	September 2009	1,002	± 3.2 percentage points
OmniPoll™ 2-09	July 2009	1,000	± 3.2 percentage points
OmniPoll™ F-08	November 2008	1,203	± 2.9 percentage points
OmniPoll™ 4-08	October 2008	1,005	± 3.2 percentage points
OmniPoll™ 3-08	August 2008	1,004	± 3.2 percentage points
OmniPoll™ 2-08	August 2008	1,003	± 3.2 percentage points
OmniPoll™ S-08	May 2008	1,003	± 3.2 percentage points
OmniPoll™ 1-08	January 2008	1,006	± 3.2 percentage points
OmniPoll™ W-07	January 2007	1,003	± 3.2 percentage points
OmniPoll™ F-07	December 2007	1,005	± 3.2 percentage points
OmniPoll™ 2-07	August 2007	1,000	± 3.2 percentage points
OmniPoll™ 1-07	January 2007	1,003	± 3.2 percentage points

When researchers describe the accuracy of survey results, the estimated amount of sampling error is often provided. This refers to the degree of inaccuracy that might be attributable to interviewing a group of people that is not completely representative of the population from which they were drawn. The maximum amount of sampling accuracy is listed in the table above. That estimate is dependent upon two factors: 1) the sample size and 2) the degree to which the result you are examining is close to 50 percent or the extremes, 0 percent and 100 percent. Keep in mind that there is a range of other errors that may influence survey results (e.g., biased question wording, question sequencing, inaccurate recording of the response provided, inaccurate data tabulation, etc.)—errors whose influence cannot be statistically estimated.

ABOUT THE AUTHOR

George Barna has filled executive roles in politics, marketing, advertising, media development, research and ministry. He founded the Barna Research Group in 1984 (now The Barna Group) and helped it become a leading marketing research firm focused on the intersection of faith and culture. His research has focused on a wide variety of topics, including faith, leadership, cultural trends, family and child development, worldview development, and transformation. In addition to playing a continuing role in The Barna Group, he is the principal in Metaformation, a company dedicated to helping people optimize their life journey, and a Senior Partner in Strategenius Group, which provides strategic marketing and business development services.

To date, Barna has written (or co-authored) more than 40 books. They include best-sellers such as *Revolution, Transforming Children into Spiritual Champions, The Frog in the Kettle, Pagan Christianity?* and *The Power of Vision.* He regularly writes analyses for *The Barna Update*, the popular online research report, and publishes a blog (www.georgebarna.com).

A popular speaker at ministry conferences around the world, Barna has been on the faculty at several universities and seminaries. He has served as a pastor of a large, multi-ethnic church, in several church start-ups, and as a house church leader.

After graduating summa cum laude from Boston College, Barna earned two master's degrees from Rutgers University. He also has a doctorate from Dallas Baptist University.

George lives with his wife and daughters in Southern California. He enjoys writing, reading novels, playing guitar and listening to music, rooting for the Yankees and Lakers, and relaxing on the beach.